240 WAYS

PRESENTS:

REALISTIC STRATEGIES THAT ERADICATE SCHOOL TO PRISON PIPELINE

MDonnel Tenner, M.Ed
"A Voice for the Children"

"A MUST READ BY THE PEOPLE"

240 Ways

Presents

Realistic Strategies That Eradicate School To PRISON PIPELINE

MDonnell Tenner, M.ED

240 Ways Presents Realistic Strategies School to Prison Pipeline

© Copyright 2018 by 240 Ways Series LLC

All Rights Reserved. No part of this book may be used or reproduced in any manner whatsoever without the expressed written permission of the Author. Address all inquiries to:
MDonnell Tenner, M.ED
240waysSeries@Gmail.com
Telephone: 314.443.8776
WWW.240wayseries.com
ISBN: 978-1546300601

Library of Congress # in progress

Cover:

Interior design: Otto Dimitrijevics

Every attempt has been made to properly source all quotes and references. Printed in the United States of America
First Edition 10 12 14 16 17 18
For additional copies of this book, please see the Quick Order Form at the back of the book or you may email 240waysSeries@gmail.com
Copyright © 2018 MDonnell Tenner All rights reserved.
ISBN-13: 978-1546300601
ISBN-10: 1546300600

DEDICATION

To the Men and Women of color that are being profiled and killed for no other reason than their skin color and lack of financial depth.

I HEAR YOU!

THE REVOLUTION WILL BE TELEVISED!

Contents

DEDICATION 5
ACKNOWLEDGEMENTS 8
REALITY 9
FOREWORD 11
PREFACE 12
INTRO 13
CHAPTER 1 14
Mistaken Belief 14
You, Me and Statistics: The Truth 22
CHAPTER 2 23
Are they building Prisons based on your ability to read? 23
   Risks of Being a Player 23
   Incarceration Trends in America 29
   Racial Disparities in Incarceration 29
   Drug Sentencing Disparities 30
CHAPTER 3 32
The three Life Killers 32
CHAPTER 4 41
Unheard-of ways to achieve greater reading 41
Tips for Making the Transition to College 50
CHAPTER 5 56
Professional Athletics is Not Your Ticket to Success 56
6 Steps to Better Grades 63
CHAPTER 6 76
Why you need a change in your environment 76

CHAPTER 7	82
Making Your Dreams a Reality	82
Chapter 8	93
One Word: High School Graduation!	93
CHAPTER 8	105
Make your college acceptance a reality	105
Do You Need A Typical Award Package?	108
EPILOGUE	**111**
ABOUT ME	**112**

ACKNOWLEDGEMENTS

Giving Honor to my Lord and Savior Jesus Christ, I say thank you for your unwavering Mercy and Grace.

To My HERO MY Mother I Love YOU!

REALITY

- Nearly 30 percent of U.S. inner-city youths are affected by "Hood Disease" which is closely associated with PTSD. Kids in the hood are exposed to Hood Disease all their lives.
- In Oakland, about two-thirds of the murders last year were actually clustered in East Oakland, where 59 people were killed.
- "Youth living in inner cities show a higher prevalence of post-traumatic stress disorder than soldiers," according to Howard Spivak M.D., director of the U.S Centers for Disease Control and Prevention's Division of Violence Prevention.
- "Its kids are unsafe, they're not well fed," Duncan-Andrade said. "And when you start stacking those kids of stressors on top of each other, that's when you get these kinds of negative mental health outcomes that seriously disrupt school performance."
- "These are the cards that [students] are suddenly wearing around their necks that say 'Rest in peace.' You have some kids that are walking around with six of them. Laminated cards that are tributes to their slain friends," said teacher Jasmine Miranda.
- ☐ "In the real world where these affects real lives, people are suffering from a chronic level of trauma that doesn't have a chance to heal because they're effectively living in a war zone within your town," said Simmons.
- Dr. Jeff Duncan-Andrade of San Francisco University told CNN Los Angeles affiliate KPIX that, "You could take anyone who is experiencing the symptoms of PTSD, and the things we are currently emphasizing in school will fall off their radar. Because, frankly, it does not matter in biology class, if they don't survive the walk home."

- ✓ These people are essentially living in combat zones. Unlike soldiers, children in the inner city never leave the combat zone and often experience trauma repeatedly.
- ✓ If you're facing the stress of being hungry and the prospect of not eating once you get home, school doesn't really matter at that time.
- ✓ These people are essentially living in combat zones. Unlike soldiers, children in the inner city never leave the combat zone and often experience trauma repeatedly.
- ✓ If you worry about dying on your way home from school, reading, writing and mathematics don't really matter much at the moment. Gun violence is only one of the traumas or stressors in concentrated areas of deep poverty.

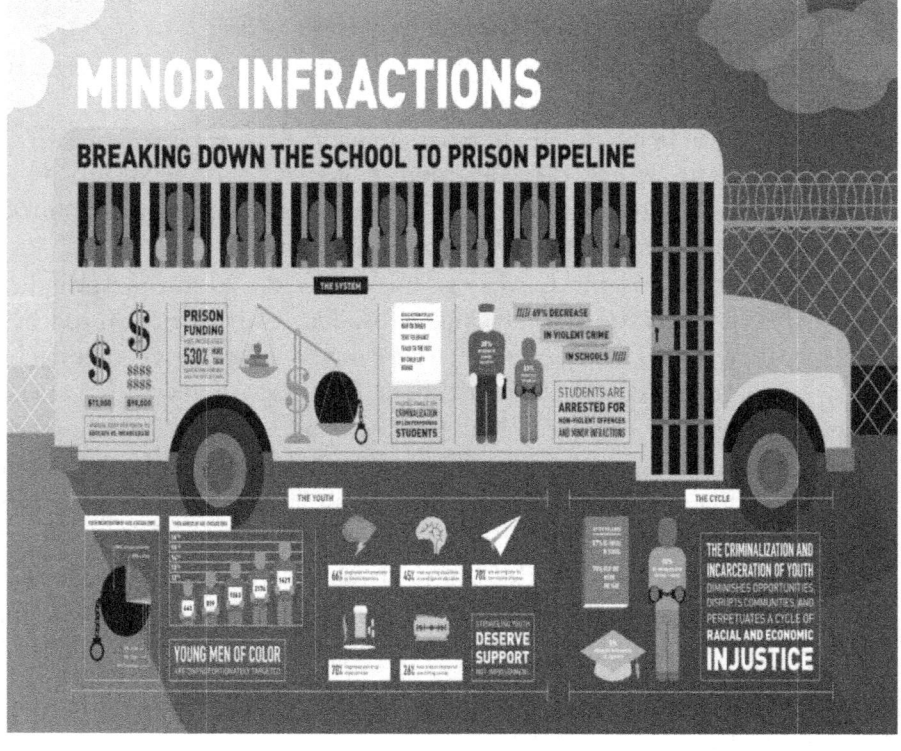

FOREWORD

Your FAITH will take you further than your RESUME!

-Chester Jackson

PREFACE

Have you ever thought about how a 2 second decision / reaction can change your life forever? Whether it is pulling a trigger, starting your car while intoxicated? Selling drugs or striking someone with your fist while in an angry rage? Have you ever thought about how your life would have been different had you stopped and thought about the repercussions of what you were about to do, the pluses and minus of the decision and what you have to lose?

I ask you today to develop a relationship with GOD. The only way that you will be able to do this is by asking GOD to come into your heart and repent your sins and ask for forgiveness. I am a witness! God will hold you, love you and answer your prayers in his time and according to his word.

INTRO

Many of you reading this book will say not me it won't happen to me. Did you know that the government has statistics that indicate what students will be going to jail based on their behavioral incidents and reading level.

THE United States Judicial System believes in Guilty till Proven INNOCENT!

They HAVE a CELL with your NAME on it

CHAPTER 1

Mistaken Belief

– Drugs Are NOT Just a One-Time Thing

Jonathan Brown is a drug awareness counselor who helps teenagers and younger adults deal with the temptation to try drugs and the constant exposure to drugs in their daily lives. Jonathan wasn't always a counselor; in fact, he was called to do this kind of work because of what happened to him. In college, Jonathan was a great athlete. He played football and he was quickly becoming the star of the team. He was also very smart and excelled academically. However, because he was quite popular, he was friends with almost everyone. This includes the 'not-so-desirable' crowd.

"Our greatest weaknes lies in giving up. The mos certain way to succeed i always to try just one mor time."
– Thomas A. Edison

One day some of Jonathan's friends from this particular crowd decided to smoke marijuana outside by the pool. Of course, they asked Jonathan to join in. At first he was reluctant but they continued to pressure him, using things like, "It's just a one-time thing to see if you like it," and "Come on, man. It's just pot." Finally, Jonathan broke down and tried it. Sure, it was just this one time and it was no big deal. But, it was a big deal. It started with a few meetings a week by the pool to smoke a little pot. Then it turned into an everyday thing. Jonathan missed practice more than once and was on very thin ice with the coach. Then, he began missing classes as well.

He spent a lot of his college money on purchasing marijuana for his friends and himself. Things continued like this for a while. Then one of his friends showed up at his apartment with something else. Rather than just smoking the same thing over and over, he had decided to buy some 'acid' or LSD. Jonathan was so high on marijuana that he didn't think twice about taking the LSD. Unfortunately, he took it without knowing the effects or what to expect. After about an hour, Jonathan began having a very bad hallucination and made so much noise in the apartment that a neighbor called the police. His friend was busy trying to 'talk him down' and the commotion only got worse when the officer knocked on the door.

Of course, from there things got even worse. There were drugs present in the apartment and both guys got arrested. Unfortunately, Jonathan was kicked off the football team and left college. His future was ruined from those few months of drugs that started off as a 'one-time thing.' Now, Jonathan works to show college athletes, as well as others, how drugs can begin as a onetime thing and lead to serious problems and consequences. Never think that drugs are a one-time thing and understand that although you may not be arrested or harmed right away, they can ruin your life and the future that you're building.

What percentage of kids aged 12 and over do you think have tried illicit drugs at least once in their lives? Ten percent? Twenty percent? Thirty percent? It's actually much, much higher. In 2013, 48.6% of kids 12 and older reported using drugs. For young people between the ages of 18 and 25, that number rises to 57%.[1] No doubt, many of these young people figured it was okay to try drugs "just this once," just like Jonathan did. You may have friends that try to tell you that it's okay to try drugs or that no one is going to find out. They may tell you to take one sip, one hit, or one drag and that it won't hurt anything.

But as Jonathan's story shows, drugs are never a one-time thing. What might start out as occasional or recreational use of a drug can turn into daily use real fast. Starting with marijuana, tobacco, or alcohol can lead to other drug use as well, including much harder drugs like cocaine. This is why marijuana is called a "gateway drug" – it opens the door to using much more dangerous drugs. In fact, kids between the ages of 12 and 17 who try marijuana, tobacco, and alcohol are up to 266 times more likely to try cocaine.[2]

---

1 "National Survey on Drug Abuse and Health," National Institute on Drug Abuse, accessed 08 Jan 2015, http://www.drugabuse.gov/national-surveydrug-use-health.[1]

2 "National Study Shows 'Gateway' Drugs Lead to Cocaine Use," Columbia University Record, accessed 08 Jan 2015, http://www.columbia.edu/cu/record/archives/vol20/vol20_iss10/record2010.24.html.[2]

As if the danger of becoming a regular drug user isn't enough, the fact is that the leading cause of crime among youth is drugs and alcohol. The leading cause of teen suicide is drugs and alcohol. Everyday kids just like you are dying because of their drug use. More than 23 million people in this country above the age of 12 are addicted to drugs or alcohol.[3] Their addiction doesn't just impact them, however. It impacts their moms and dads, aunts and uncles, brothers, sisters, and friends. So that split-second decision to take that joint or to drive drunk not only has huge impacts on your life, but on the lives of all the people you love as well.

There are many long-term impacts of a decision to try drugs "just this once." Inmates convicted of a drug offense comprise 48.7% of all inmates in federal prison.[4] Nearly 100,000 people are behind bars because they got involved with drugs by thinking that their first experience would be their last. But the relationship between drugs and crime is much more far reaching. More than one-quarter of victims of violent crime–assault, battery, and rape, among others–report that the aggressor was under the influence of drugs or alcohol at the time of the crime. Among inmates, 32% of state prisoners and 26% of federal prisoners report having been under the influence of drugs at the time of their offense.[5] In short, drugs don't just lead to a night in jail and a misdemeanor drug charge. They lead to crimes against women, carjacking, home invasions, property destruction, and all kinds of other violent crimes.

Using drugs, even just once, can have long-term effects on your brain as well. When someone uses drugs, the chemistry in his or her brain changes. With repeated use of drugs, those changes become more pronounced. Over time, a person can develop tolerance to their drug of choice. This means that they require more and more of the drug to achieve the same high they did the first time they used it. So while smoking one joint might get someone as high as a kite the first time, the second, third, and fourth times they will need more of the drug to get the same experience.

After repeated use, drug users can also begin to develop cravings. These cravings can even be seen in brain scans. If someone who is addicted to cocaine

---

[3] "Frequently Asked Questions and Facts," National Council on Alcoholism and Drug Dependence, accessed 08 Jan 2015, https://ncadd.org/for-youth/ facts.[3]

[4] "Inmate Statistics: Offenses," Federal Bureau of Prisons, 29 Nov 2014, accessed on 09 Jan 2015, http://www.bop.gov/about/statistics/statistics_inmate_offenses.jsp.[4]

[5] "Drugs and Crimes Facts," Bureau of Justice Statistics, accessed 09 Jan 2015, http://www.bjs.gov/content/dcf/duc.cfm#to.

sees a picture of drug paraphernalia, the part of his or her brain responsible for emotional memory, the amygdala, is activated and a strong craving for cocaine is reported.[6] This occurs without cocaine even being present – just a picture of a pipe is enough to get their body craving the drug. This is why quitting drugs is so hard to do. The brain becomes so used to having the substance in the body that it keeps begging for more.

When someone uses drugs, it can greatly impact their loved ones. Family members can experience a range of feelings, from abandonment and anxiety to anger and fear. A member of the family that uses drugs might find him or herself isolated from the rest of the family and all alone. Sometimes drug users forget about their family altogether, choosing instead to spend time with other users who reinforce their drug using behaviors.

The cost and expense of drugs can take a heavy toll on families as family members grow to resent their loved one for spending money on drugs and not on food, rent, and other necessities. Little brothers and sisters learn inappropriateate norms for acceptable behavior from older siblings that choose to use. Children that see their parents abusing drugs lack a positive role model to help them learn and grow in a positive manner. Trust can become a serious issue between husbands and wives when one party takes to using drugs.[7] On so many levels–interpersonal, social, emotional, financial, and physical – drugs serve to tear down families and ruin relationships.

The only way to protect yourself from the dangers of drugs is never to try them in the first place! You can't get addicted if you refuse to try drugs. You can't get busted for possession if you don't carry drugs around. You can't drive drunk if you don't take that first drink. Your decision to use drugs or alcohol for the first time isn't just a one-time thing. It is a decision that can have long-term negative impacts on your physical health, the wellness of your family, and your freedom.

But drugs are just one aspect of a larger group of issues: Urban Life Misconceptions. These misconceptions revolve around the idea that the fast life and making easy money is the ticket to a better life for yourself, when the true

---

[6] "Long-Term Effects of Drugs on the Brain," National Institutes of Health, 2009, accessed 09 Jan 2015, https://science.education.nih.gov/supplements/nih2/addiction/guide/pdfs/master4.6.pdf.

[7] Substance Abuse and Mental Health Services Administration, Treatment Improvement Protocol, Chapter 2: Impact of Substance Abuse on Families. Rockville, MD: Center for Substance Abuse Treatment, 2004. http://www.ncbi.nlm.nih.gov/books/NBK64258/.

ticket to a good life is getting an education. Which sounds better: Doing something illegal to make some quick cash to tide you over for a few weeks or months at a time, or having a steady income that will add up to hundreds of thousands of dollars over your lifetime?

Sure, getting into the drug scene as a dealer or stealing and fencing jewelry will get you fast cash, but think also of all the negative aspects of living that life – violence, guns, gang activity, and always having to look over your shoulder for the cops or a rival gang member. That's not to mention the hurt and pain those activities inflict on the victims of crime and their families. But sometimes in desperate situations, it might seem like the fast life is the only way to get the money you need to survive. This interaction between crime and poverty serves to keep many young men of color out of school where they belong and stuck in alternating states of unemployment and imprisonment.

But trying to live the fast life has implications for your education as well. If you drop out of school to get quick cash through illegal activities, you aren't gaining the skills you need to get a real job, with long-term, stable employment opportunities. What happens if you get busted for robbery or possession? When you get out, what marketable skills would you have to get a good job and support yourself and your family? Without an education, you wouldn't have any skills and would be poverty-stricken and more easily sucked back into the game of making money illegally. This sets you up to get busted again, creating a vicious cycle in which you are in and out of jail for the rest of your life. That's why getting an education is so critical to escaping the issues of urban life.

That's easier said than done though, because unfortunately schools haven't done a good job in the past of addressing the needs of urban kids of color. Disparities in education exist along racial and socioeconomic lines, meaning students that are black or Latino and poor get the fewest educational opopportunities. As a group, black males are failed more by the educational system than any other racial or ethnic group. If you are a black student, even before you walk into kindergarteten on the first day of school, you face achievement gaps that will persist throughout your lifetime. In fact, the failures of the educational system are so bad that black boys are more likely to become residents of a prison cell than they are to be residents of a college dorm.[8]

This track from school to prison is called the school-toprison pipeline, and it has a disproportionate impact on students of color. More than two-thirds of

---

[8] "Policy Notes: News from the ETS Policy Information Center," Educational Testing Service, 2011, accessed 12 Jan 2015, http://www.ets.org/Media/Research/pdf/PIC-PNV19n3.pdf.

students who are arrested at school are black or Latino. Of all kids expelled from school each year, 40% are black. If a white student and a black student commit the exact same infraction, the black student is three times as likely to be suspended.[9] Unfortunately, these numbers probably come as no surprise.

There are a number of reasons why this school-to-prison pipeline situation exists:[10]

1. School Police: Armed police now roam the halls of schools to maintain order in classrooms and hallways. In just the last twenty years, the number of school resource officers has risen 38%. Because of this, school children, especially minority boys, are much more likely to be arrested at school than they were just a few years ago. School arrests even happen for minor offenses such as causing a classroom disruption.

2. Zero-tolerance policies: In the 1990s, zerotolerance policies became popular as a way to deter violence at school. Since then, schools at all levels, even preschools, have adopted these policies. Zerotolerance policies establish automatic punishments for unwanted behaviors, regardless of the circumstances. For example, a child who has over-the-counter allergy medication in her backpack might be kicked out of school for violating an anti-drug policy. What makes the problem worse is that a lot of the time a student's right to due process is ignored, especially if the child is a minority. This means that minority students are often treated unfairly, and their rights as a citizen and a student are not honored.

3. Juvenile court and detention: Once a student is taken out of school due to a zero-tolerance infraction or an arrest at school, they often end up in juvenile court or juvenile detention, even for offenses like having a pair of scissors in their backpack without the intention of using them for harm. Once kids reach this point, it is incredibly hard to get back into school. Banned from school grounds, kids have no safe place to go during the day, and end up poor, without an education, and without a job.

Even urban kids of color who graduate from high school do so without a lot of support for continued education or a pathway to a job with a decent

---

[9] "Fact Sheet: How Bad is the School-To-Prison Pipeline," Corporation for Public Broadcasting, 2013, accessed 13 Jan 2015, http://www.pbs.org/wnet/tavissmiley/tsr/education-under-arrest/school-to-prison-pipeline-factsheet/.

[10] "What is the School-To-Prison Pipeline?," American Civil Liberties Union, accessed 14 Jan 2015, https://www.aclu.org/racial-justice/what-schoolprison-pipeline.

wage.[11] This just means that you will have to work harder than everybody else in order to make positive changes in your life and escape the draw of the fast life and easy money. But that hard work is worth it! In 2012, workers without a high school diploma made an average of just $22,900 each year, but workers who graduated from high school or got their G.E.D. made an average annual income of $30,000.

College graduates make even more each year. With a twoyear degree, workers earn about $37,000 on average, while workers with a four-year degree earn $46,900.[12] It may not be easy money or fast money, but it is long-term, stable, and respectable money that adds up over time. In fact, the average college graduate will earn $830,000 more than a high school graduate will earn by the time they retire.[13] Upcoming chapters in this book offer great tips for getting into a position to improve yourself, starting with getting graduated from high school, going to college, and getting a good job so you can build a positive life for you and your family.

---

[11] "Challenges Facing Urban Youth," Year Up, 2008, accessed 12 Jan 2015, http://www.doleta.gov/youth_services/pdf/Year_2Page_Overview011508.pdf.

[12] "Income of Young Adults," National Center for Education Statistics, 2012, accessed 14 Jan 2015, http://nces.ed.gov/fastfacts/display.asp?id=77.

[13] "Is it Still Worth Going to College?," Federal Reserve Bank of San Francisco, 2014, accessed 12 Jan 2015, http://www.frbsf.org/economic-research/publications/economic-letter/2014/may/is-college-worth-it-educationtuition-wages/.

FROM SCHOOL TO PRISON

STUDENTS OF COLOR FACE HARSHER DISCIPLINE AND ARE MORE LIKELY TO BE PUSHED OUT OF SCHOOL THAN WHITES.

40%  OF STUDENTS EXPELLED FROM U.S. SCHOOLS EACH YEAR ARE BLACK.

70%  OF STUDENTS INVOLVED IN "IN-SCHOOL" ARRESTS OR REFERRED TO LAW ENFORCEMENT ARE BLACK OR LATINO.

3.5X  BLACK STUDENTS ARE THREE AND A HALF TIMES MORE LIKELY TO BE SUSPENDED THAN WHITES.

2X  BLACK AND LATINO STUDENTS ARE TWICE AS LIKELY TO NOT GRADUATE HIGH SCHOOL AS WHITES.

68% OF ALL MALES IN STATE AND FEDERAL PRISON DO NOT HAVE A HIGH SCHOOL DIPLOMA.

You, Me and Statistics: The Truth

I am making sure that you see the statistics and hear from someone who is just like YOU! Young, poor, Black and labeled ADHD with a single family home. I ask you to read this book, take notes and develop a plan that will take you to where you dream to be and where you ought to be.

1. 2/3 of students who cannot read proficiently by the end of 4th grade will end up in jail or on welfare. Over 70% of America's inmates cannot read above a 4th grade level.
2. 1 in 4 children in America grow up without learning how to read.
3. Students who don't read proficiently by the 3rd grade are 4 times likelier to drop out of school.
4. As of 2011, America was the only free-market OECD(Organization for Economic Cooperation and Development) country where the current generation was less educated than the previous one.
5. Nearly 85% of the juveniles who face trial in the juvenile court system are functionally illiterate, proving that there is a close relationship between illiteracy and crime. More than 60% of all inmates are functionally illiterate.
6. 53% of 4th graders admitted to reading recreationally "almost every day," while only 20% of 8th graders could say the same.
7. 75% of Americans who receive food stamps perform at the lowest 2 levels of literacy, and 90% of high school dropouts are on welfare.
8. Teenage girls between the ages of 16 to 19 who live at or below the poverty line and have below average literacy skills are 6 times more likely to have children out of wedlock than girls their age who can read proficiently.
9. Reports show that the rate of low literacy in the United States directly costs the healthcare industry over $70 million every year.
10. In 2013, Washington, D.C. was ranked the most literate American city for the third year in a row, with Seattle and Minneapolis close behind.
11. Long Beach, CA was ranked the country's most illiterate city, followed by Mesa, AZ, and Aurora, CO.

CHAPTER 2

Are they building Prisons based on your ability to read?

Risks of Being a Player

*I*n *high school, it sure seems totally cool to have been with this person or that person, to have gone this far with one and that far with another. A lot of it is just big talk from guys trying to sound like pimps, but sometimes its reality. If you're one of these guys who think it's really cool to play the pimp game, you should know about Matt. Matt was one of these guys too. He was handsome enough, which is why he was able to get close to so many people. In his friend's eyes, Matt was king at their high school until soon enough, with a twist of fate, Matt became a dad.*

> *"Out of clutter, find Simplicity. From discord, find Harmony. In the middle of difficulty lies Opportunity."*
>
> *– Albert Einstein*

Because the pregnant girl was kicked out of her home, Matt had to quit school and get a job in order to support her and their child. Matt was no longer the king of the high school. In fact, without his education, the best job Matt was able to get was helping out at a mechanic's shop that paid minimum wage. The guy he used to be was gone, and Matt's entire life, his dreams, and his goals were gone as well. If Matt's story doesn't show you the risks of playing the pimp game, perhaps Josh's story will.

Josh was very similar to Matt. He was captain of the football team, and he was very popular and well loved by the girls. With a cute face and charming demeanor, Josh could get away with many different things. His friends looked forward to his bragging sessions on Mondays after a weekend of hanging out with girls. One day very close to graduation, Josh didn't show up on Monday because he was at the doctor's office. Josh had contracted

Human Papilloma virus and had gone to the doctor when he noticed small bumps, which turned out to be genital warts.

It's bad enough to contract a sexually transmitted disease for which there is no cure. But because it can take from three months to several years to show up, Josh had to contact all of the girls that he had 'spent time' with over the past two years to inform them that he had the disease. Josh quickly went from Mr. Popular to someone who was avoided. There are many risks to playing the pimp game, and you just can't afford to take the 'it-wont-happen-to-me' attitude because it can. Don't put your whole life at risk. In Josh's case, his disease was not fatal and could be treated, although HPV is incurable. It could have been something much worse.

Unfortunately, sexually transmitted diseases are just a few of the many risks you have to think about if you're trying to be a player. If you spend all your time trying to get with girls, you won't be focused on the most important thing–getting an education. As was discussed in Chapter 1, getting an education is the key to building a better life. But that can be tough to do in urban school districts where there are often fewer resources and unfair policies that target black and Latino boys. But the importance of persevering and overcoming these obstacles is extremely important. Your level of education can have significant impacts on whether you live the life of a free man or one who spends his days in a prison cell.

A lot of research has been done trying to identify characteristics of people that might predict if they will or will not spend time in prison. One surprising finding is that there is a connection between a person's literacy level in the third grade, high school dropout rates, and risk of imprisonment. Poverty is often associated with not reading well. In fact, more than one-quarter of children who experience family poverty do not read at grade level, and 35% of kids who are poor and live in poor neighborhoods do not read proficiently. Combining those two factors together – lack of reading ability and family poverty – make it three times as likely that a student will drop out of high school or fail to graduate. More than one-third of kids that also live in a poor neighborhood fail to graduate.[14] So what does that have to do with future imprisonment?

---

[14] "Double Jeopardy: How Third Grade Reading Skills and Poverty Influence High School Graduation," City University of New York, 2012, accessed 15 Jan 2015, http://www.aecf.org/m/resourcedoc/AECF-DoubleJeopardy-2012Full.pdf.

Large numbers of children that do not read proficiently do not graduate from high school. Kids who lag behind in reading skills in elementary school are four times as likely not to graduate from high school on time. Kids that do not graduate from high school are 63 times more likely than a college graduate to be incarcerated at some point in their life.[15] So that's the connection – if you don't read well, your chances of graduating high school are less, and without graduating from high school, your chances of being imprisoned are vastly increased.

But the bad news doesn't stop there. Black and Latino kids are much more likely than white kids to live in family poverty and to live in poor neighborhoods, which increases the risk of not reading well and of not graduating from high school. In fact, children of color who do not read well and live in poverty are twice as likely to not graduate from high school as white children who do not read well and live in poverty. In short, the social and economic barriers that you face on a daily basis makes it less likely that you will graduate from high school and more likely you will spend time in prison.

Many schools, recognizing how important reading is to the future of students, but particularly students like you, have started intervention programs aimed at improving kids' reading skills. A lot of these programs focus on elementary school kids so they build the skills they need to be successful readers later in life. But interventions for middle school and high school students also exist. Primarily, the idea is to immerse students in reading so they get practice with learning vocabulary, decoding texts, and reading comprehension.[16]

So since reading is a critical component of you being a successful young man, you need to read a lot. Later in this book we'll talk about some strategies you can use to become a better reader, but a big part of doing so is just to read. One of the biggest factors in becoming a better reader is to read and read often. This doesn't mean you have to read huge novels or textbooks

> *"I don't know the key to success, but the key to failure is trying to please everybody."*
>
> – Bill Cosby

---

[15] "The Consequences of Dropping Out of High School," Northwestern University, 2009, accessed 15 Jan 2015, http://www.northeastern.edu/clms/ wp-content/uploads/The_Consequences_of_Dropping_Out_of_High_ School.pdf.

[16] "A Call for Change: Providing Solutions for Black Male Achievement," Council of the Great City Schools, 2012, accessed 17 Jan 2015, http://files.eric.ed.gov/full text/ED539625.pdf.

all the time (although those should be part of it). Read the labels on your clothes, the ads at the bus stop, and the nutritional information on your food. Read anything and everything you can get your hands on because every little bit that you read each day will improve your skills.

Another factor that works against you as a black or Latino student is the disproportionate number of suspensions and expulsions that black and Latino students face at school. As discussed in Chapter 1, the largest percentage of students expelled each year are black, and a black student is three times as likely to be suspended from school as a white student that commits the exact same infraction. Latino students are 1.5 times as likely as a white student to be suspended and almost twice as likely to be expelled.[17] So already being at-risk for not completing high school, you have to go to school in an educational system that targets you for removal from school, increasing that much more the likelihood that you won't graduate.

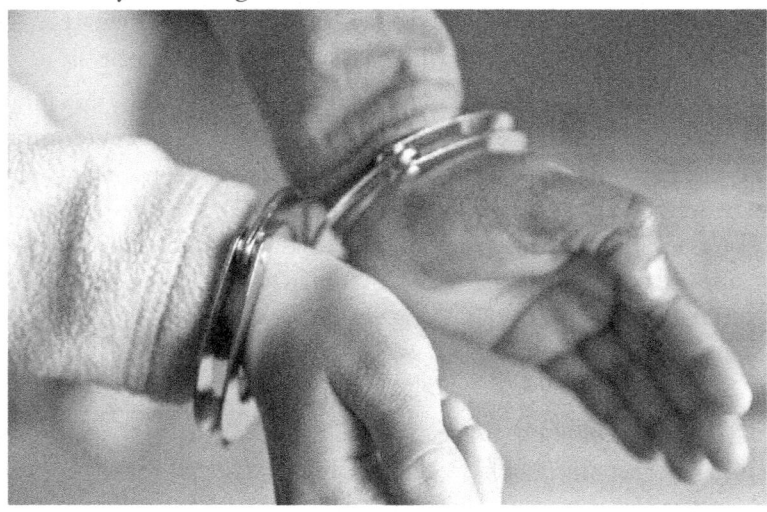

"You are The Company You KEEP"
"Your income will be the average of your 3 closes friends"

This is where the relationship between school suspensions/expulsions and prison is revealed. Because of strict zero tolerance policies in schools, even the

---

[17] "Pushed Out," Teaching Tolerance, 2009, accessed 15 Jan 2015, http://www.tolerance.org/pushed-out.

most minor infractions can send a student to the juvenile justice system, and sometimes even the adult criminal justice system. Crazy stories have emerged from all over the country about children being arrested or charged with crimes for minor offenses:[18]

1) In Colorado, an 11-year-old boy was charged with misdemeanor theft for taking a lollipop off his teacher's desk. He was convicted and placed on probation.
2) In Florida, a five-year-old girl was removed from school by police and arrested for having a temper tantrum.
3) In Georgia, a teenager was expelled from school for talking on his cell phone, even after it was learned he was talking to his mother who was deployed in Iraq at the time. It was the first time in a month they were able to speak.

These cases illustrate how modern school discipline policies are out of control. Removing you from school does not help you learn, particularly if you are a black or Latino student and already facing disadvantages that negatively impact learning. But, as bleak as it may seem, there are positive steps being taken to correct the faults of the educational system that impact your ability to succeed.

A lot of attention has been paid to zero tolerance policies in schools, and how they target children of color and do so with unnecessary force. Many school districts have replaced harsh zero tolerance policies with programs that discipline students with in-school suspension, where they continue to work on their school assignments under the direction of a certified teacher, rather than being expelled and removed from school.[19] Another popular intervention offers behavioral supports for kids who are at-risk of misbehavior due to social, economic, personal, or other factors. Rather than punishing students who may or may not be familiar with school behavioral policies, under this intervention, students take part in learning exercises to develop a better understanding of

---

[18] "Pushed Out," Teaching Tolerance, 2009, accessed 15 Jan 2015, http://www.tolerance.org/pushed-out.

[19] "Education or Incarceration: Zero Tolerance Policies and the School to Prison Pipeline," Forum on Public Policy, 2009, accessed 16 Jan 2015, http://files.eric.ed.gov/full text/EJ870076.pdf.

their emotions and learn ways to interact with their teachers and peers in a more appropriate manner.[20]

There has also been a shift in many schools towards utilizing positive reinforcement and interventions to encourage responsible behavior. Students, teachers, and staff members all participate in such programs, which make changes to everything from what is taught and how, to how teachers organize and structure their classrooms. But the biggest changes come in the way in which schools handle discipline, which goes from being reactive to being responsive. Rather than reacting when students mess up by suspending or expelling them, schools take an active approach to teaching positive behaviors and meeting the individual needs of each student.

For example, a big part of these programs is to focus on praising students for the good things they do. When you hand in your homework on time, hold the door open for a classmate, help someone pick up a book they dropped, or anything else that is positive or responsible, you get recognized for it. It might just be a simple "thank you" or a pat on the back from your teacher, but the point is that there is a much greater emphasis on acknowledging all the good things you do throughout the day for yourself and for other people. By promoting positive behaviors and recognizing when they occur, the whole school environment changes from being focused on what goes wrong to being focused on what everyone is doing right.[21]

> *"Nonviolence is the answer to the crucial political and moral questions of our time: the need for man to overcome oppression and violence without resorting to oppression and violence. Man must evolve for all human conflict a method which rejects revenge, aggression, and retaliation. The foundation of such method is love."*
>
> – Martin Luther King Jr.

It may sound a little crazy that focusing on positive behavior would have that much of an effect on the school environment. But it does! Research shows that schools that use this kind of intervention have a huge decrease in the number of discipline referrals,

---

[20] "Zero Tolerance Policies and the Public Schools: When Suspension is No Longer Effective," National Association of School Psychologists, accessed 16 Jan 2015, http://www.nasponline.org/publications/cq/37/5/zerotolerance.aspx.

[21] "Positive Behavioral Supports: Information for Educators," National Association of School Psychologists, 2001, accessed 17 Jan 2015, http://www.nasponline.org/resources/factsheets/pbs_fs.aspx.

sometimes by as much as 80-90% from one year to the next. Imagine going to a school where you don't have to be afraid of getting suspended or expelled all the time! Sounds good, right?

Let's be clear: you have to be responsible for your behavior. You have to go to school each day, do your work, be respectful, and do what you need to do to graduate. That can be really hard, especially when you might come from a poor family or a poor neighborhood or go to a school that doesn't have a lot of resources to help you learn. But, if you do your part, and the school does their part to help you along the way, you will be much more likely to stay in school and be successful. Later in this book you'll learn some strategies that will help you hold up your end of the bargain at school. You'll learn about how you can become a better reader, how to study better, and how to deal with the stress from school so you can grow to improved things in your life.

"Over 70% of the incarcerated are ILLITERATE: Can't read and or write at grade level"

"If your friends are doing wrong and you are hanging with them sooner or later you will be doing the wrongs that they are doing"

Incarceration Trends in America

- From 1980 to 2008, the number of people incarcerated in America quadrupled-from roughly 500,000 to 2.3 million people Today, the US is 5% of the World population and has 25% of world prisoners.
- Combining the number of people in prison and jail with those under parole or probation supervision, 1 in ever y 31 adults, or 3.2 percent of the population is under some form of correctional control

Racial Disparities in Incarceration

- African Americans now constitute nearly 1 million of the total
- 2.3 million incarcerated population African Americans are incarcerated at nearly six times the rate of whites Together, African American and Hispanics comprised 58% of all prisoners in 2008, even though African

Americans and Hispanics make up approximately one quarter of the US population
- According to Unlocking America, if African American and Hispanics were incarcerated at the same rates of whites, today's prison and jail populations would decline by approximately 50%
- One in six black men had been incarcerated as of 2001. If current trends continue, one in three black males born today can expect to spend time in prison during his lifetime 1 in 100 African American women are in prison
- Nationwide, African-Americans represent 26% of juvenile ar-rests, 44% of youth who are detained, 46% of the youth who are judicially waived to criminal court, and 58% of the youth admitted to state prisons (Center on Juvenile and Criminal Justice).

Drug Sentencing Disparities

- About 14 million Whites and 2.6 million African Americans report using an illicit drug.
- 5 times as many Whites are using drugs as African Americans, yet African Americans are sent to prison for drug offenses at 10 times the rate of Whites.
- African Americans represent 12% of the total population of drug users, but 38% of those arrested for drug offenses, and 59% of those in state prison for a drug offense.
- African Americans serve virtually as much time in prison for a drug offense (58.7 months) as whites do for a violent offense (61.7 months). (Sentencing Project)

Contributing Factors

- ✓ Inner city crime prompted by social and economic isolation
- ✓ Crime/drug arrest rates:
- ✓ African Americans represent 12% of monthly drug users, but comprise 32% of persons arrested for drug possession "Get tough on crime" and "war on drugs" policies Mandatory minimum sentencing, especially disparities in sentencing for crack and powder cocaine possession

- ✓ In 2002, blacks constituted more than 80% of the people sentenced under the federal crack cocaine laws and served substantially more time in prison for drug offenses than did whites, despite that fact that more than 2/3 of crack cocaine users in the U.S. are white or Hispanic
- ✓ "Three Strikes"/habitual offender policies
- ✓ Zero Tolerance policies as a result of perceived problems of school violence; adverse effect on black children.
- ✓ 35% of black children grades 7-12 have been suspended or expelled at some point in their school careers compared to 20% of Hispanics and 15% of whites

Effects of Incarceration

- ✓ Jail reduces work time of young people over the next decade by 25-30 percent when compared with arrested youths who were not incarcerated
- ✓ Jails and prisons are recognized as settings where society's infectious diseases are highly concentrated
- ✓ Prison has not been proven as a rehabilitation for behavior, as two-thirds of prisoners will reoffend

Exorbitant Cost of Incarceration: Is it Worth It?

- ✓ About $70 billion dollars are spent on corrections yearly
- ✓ Prisons and jails consume a growing portion of the nearly $200 billion we spend annually on public safety

"Missouri passes a law in 2016 that if you are a student and you get into a fight you can and will be charged with a FELONY!"

CHAPTER 3

The three Life Killers

What is the Right Crowd?

College athletes are a unique breed. They are generally quite popular and have friends from many different social groups. Girls love them; guys want to be them. However, it's quite easy to fall into the wrong crowd and end up being not so great! Jared knows all

> "With the new day comes new strength and new thoughts."
> – Eleanor Roosevelt

about this, as he ended up in the wrong crowd. Here's a bit more about what happened to Jared.

Jared didn't know anyone when he started college hundreds of miles away from home. He had the football team, but everyone was quite new, so they weren't really friends yet. Jared was a very good student. He was self-motivated, academically gifted, hardworking and more. He was the kind of high school student who any teacher would love to have in class, and he hoped that proved to be the case in college. However, Jared's roommate was of a different kind of unique. He was a procrastinator and barely seemed to slide by in high school. He didn't have very high ambitions, and most of his time was spent with girls at parties.

As Jared got to know Keith a bit better, he began to go to different parties with him and spend more time with him. However, Jared noticed that Keith had no time designated for studying or classes. As Jared would just crack a book to begin studying, Keith would run in *saying they needed to go to a particular party or that some really cute girls were coming over. Jared couldn't seem to find time to do anything. He was having fun, but he was letting his studies slip, and he felt guilty. Before too long, the parties and the procrastination started showing up in his grades. Finally, Jared realized that enough was enough.*

In high school, Jared's friends were very similar to him. They all had high goals, they valued education and learning and they wanted to make a great career out of the things they loved. Jared realized that when he had spent time with those friends, they had fun in a different way than he and Keith did. So, he started finding friends more like the ones he had back in high school. He felt good when he finally got to know some people with similar interests. He had forgotten how motivating friends could be for each other.

Jared and his new friends studied together and challenged each other to be better, stronger and faster. It was a very rewarding relationship, and they learned a lot from each other. In no time, his grades were back to top-notch, and when Keith wanted to go to a party, Jared stayed home. He felt as if he had accomplished something, and knowing that his friends were of the same mindset, he did wonderfully. Keith, on the other hand, failed and left college. He is now paid minimum wage for a very stressful job that he doesn't enjoy. The moral of the story? Stay focused and surround yourself with like-minded individuals, and you will succeed!

The crowd you get in with can help determine what kind of life you will lead. In the wrong crowd, you could easily end up leading a life of violence, drugs, gangs, prison and other "life killers." But at the same time, if the company you keep is made up of other good people trying to make something of themselves, you will be better equipped to avoid all the pitfalls of being in with the wrong crowd. That's not to say that you aren't ultimately responsible for the choices you make, but having positive influences in your life will definitely make good decision-making a whole lot easier.

Living in an urban environment can be a lot like living in a war zone. You undoubtedly known someone that has committed a crime or been imprisoned, that's a member of a gang, who has fallen victim to drug use, or has been shot, stabbed, or experienced some other kind of violence. Chances are, someone you know, someone that is close to you and whom you love, has had one of these negative experiences. If this is the case, know that you aren't alone.

The statistics for life killers in urban areas are sobering. There are, on average, nearly 460 violent crimes per 100,000 people committed in urban areas each year. This includes more than five murders, 28 rapes, over 152 robberies, and more than 273 aggravated assaults per 100,000 residents. Compare those numbers with violent crime statistics for areas like the suburbs, where there are 396 violent crimes per 100,000 people, including four murders, 63 robberies, and 288 aggravated assaults. Those numbers are even lower for rural communities, which experience just over 202 violent crimes per 100,000 people.[22] Your neighborhood might be better than the average, or it could be even worse. The point is, avoiding life killers can be hard when you live in an environment that is home to so many life killers in the first place.

But the statistics discussed above don't even begin to scratch the surface, because not only do you have to worry about becoming a victim of a crime, you also have to worry about being the one perpetrating the crimes. In Chapter 1, we discussed some of the dangers of drugs and how they are not just a one-time thing. You learned about how drugs can negatively impact your body and your mind, your family relationships, and your freedom. The last part – your freedom

– is at risk if you use drugs, but it is at extraordinary risk if you get involved in selling drugs.

Approximately 17.5% of all drug arrests in the United States are for the manufacture, sale, or distribution of drugs.[23] Heroin, cocaine, and marijuana are the three drugs people are most often arrested for selling. People convicted of dealing heroin face a minimum prison sentence of five years if the amount involved is less than a kilogram. If the amount involved is more than a kilogram, the minimum mandatory sentence is ten years. The same sentences apply for cocaine: if the defendant trafficked less than five kilograms, the sentence is five years,

---

[22] "Crimes and Crime Rates by Type of Offense: 1980-2009," U.S. Census Bureau, 2012, accessed 18 Jan 2015, http://www.census.gov/compendia/statab/2012/tables/12s0307.pdf.

[23] "Drugs and Crime Facts," Bureau of Justice Statistics, 2007, accessed 18 Jan 2015, http://www.bjs.gov/content/dcf/enforce.cfm.

but if the amount was more than five kilograms, the sentence is ten years.

If someone is arrested again for dealing heroin or cocaine, the penalties become stricter. The penalties for smaller amounts of the drug go up to a minimum 10-year sentence, while for larger amounts of the drug the penalty is a minimum of 20 years behind bars. If someone loses their life or experiences severe injuries because of the drugs, the defendant could go to jail for the rest of his or her life.[24] The prison sentences just keep getting longer the more times someone is convicted of dealing and the more people that are hurt by the drugs they deal.

> "The only justification for ever looking down on somebody is to pick them up."
> – Jesse Jackson

The next time your "friend" asks you to hold his dime bag, or your girlfriend asks you to help her sell some weed, or your neighbor convinces you to run money for drugs, think about the consequences of your decision. Mandatory minimum sentences are no joke. You could lose five, 10, or 20 years of your life in an instant. And if you don't learn your lesson the first time, you might never experience the joy of free life ever again. Is the quick, easy money really worth it?

Some kids in urban areas get involved in violence and crime because they join a gang. Sometimes they join of their own accord, but sometimes it might be expected of them because their dad, brother, uncle, or friend is a gang member. A lot of times kids join gangs because they feel like doing so offers them protection from violence at school or in the community. Still other kids get involved in the gang life because they think it gives them some kind of high status in the neighborhood, or because they think it will get them more money than having a legitimate job.[25]

Gangs used to be associated with assaults, robberies, murder, and drugs. But today, gangs are becoming increasingly violent and expanding their illegal activities to include human trafficking,

---

[24] "Federal Trafficking Penalties for Schedules I, II, III, IV, and V," U.S. Drug Enforcement Administration, accessed 19 Jan 2015, http://www.dea.gov/druginfo/ftp3.shtml.

[25] "Changing Course: Keeping Kids Out of Gangs," National Institute of Justice, accessed 20 Jan 2015, https://ncjrs.gov/pdffiles1/nij/244146.pdf.

prostitution, extortion, gun smuggling, and international drug trafficking. The truly scary part is that gangs are becoming younger, with more and more teenagers joining up in recent years. In fact, many states across the nation report that juvenile gang members perpetrate the majority of gang-related crime and violence.[26]

This is why it is vital for you to be mindful of the company you keep. Someone that asks you to hide their drugs, forces you to join a gang, or encourages you to engage in criminal activity is not your friend! They do not care about you. But with so many people in your neighborhood participating in life killing activities, and all the violence and crime in urban areas, how can you avoid falling into the trap of life killers?

There are many positive influences you can surround yourself with that will give you the opportunity to rise above your surroundings and make something special out of your life. Mentoring programs like Big Brothers Big Sisters pair kids with positive adult role models who talk with kids, help them with homework, and otherwise spend time with kids after school and on the weekends. Research shows that these programs have a positive effect on youth in a number of different areas of life, including improved school performance, social skills, overall attitude, and emotional wellness.[27]

School is another place where you can find positive support. Maybe you have a favorite teacher that inspires you to learn, or perhaps the principal at your school is a good role model for you. Maybe you have friends at school from a different neighborhood that want more for their life just like you do. Whoever you look up to or hang out with at school, make sure they are of like mind and spirit to you – you can lean on them for support and guidance. They can also encourage you to stay in school and get your diploma. Remember, kids that do not graduate from high school are 63 times more likely than a college

---

[26] "2011 National Gang Threat Assessment," Federal Bureau of Investigation, 2011, accessed 19 Jan 2015, http://www.fbi.gov/stats-services/ publications/2011-national-gang-threat-assessment.

[27] "Vulnerable Youth: Federal Mentoring Programs and Issues," Congressional Research Service, 2012, accessed 20 Jan 2015, https://www.fas.org/sgp/crs/misc/RL34306.pdf.

graduate to be incarcerated at some point in their life, so an education is a key component of staying away from life killers.

Many kids are finding that there are a lot of people right in their own backyard who can be positive influences and sources of strength. Maybe you don't have a mom or dad at home, or perhaps you have older siblings that have gotten in trouble with the law. But that doesn't mean that you don't have other family members, friends, or neighbors who you can lean on for support. In fact, many urban neighborhoods are coming together to take part in community-based programs that seek to help support kids in just this way. By working together, urban neighborhoods are providing the support system that kids like you need – people that care about you, teach you valuable skills, make sure you go to school, and look out for you on the playground, in the street, or in your backyard.[28] This overall sense of shared belonging and purpose goes a long way in pushing out the life killers.

Urban life can be bleak sometimes, but even though it may seem like you can't escape the drugs, the gangs, and the violence, you can! Staying in school, having a mentor, and surrounding yourself with positive influences can all have a huge impact on the course your life takes. It might be the hardest decision of your life to leave your friends behind when they get involved in life killing activities. But the alternative – a life of crime, followed by a life behind bars – isn't worth it!

1. **While people of color make up about 30 percent of the United States' population, they account for 60 percent of those imprisoned.** The prison population grew by 700 percent from 1970 to 2005, a rate that is outpacing crime and population rates. The incarceration rates disproportionately impact men of color: 1 in every 15 African American men and 1 in every 36 Hispanic men are incarcerated in comparison to 1 in every 106 white men.
2. **According to the Bureau of Justice Statistics, one in three black men can expect to go to prison in their lifetime.** Individuals of color have a disproportionate number of encounters with law enforcement, indicating that racial profiling continues to be a problem. A report by the Department of Justice found that

---

[28] "The Positive Effects of Youth Community Engagement," Texas School Safety Center, 2013, accessed 19 Jan 2015, http://txssc.txstate.edu/topics/ youth-leadership/articles/positive-effects-of-youth-engagement.

blacks and Hispanics were approximately three times more likely to be searched during a traffic stop than white motorists. African Americans were twice as likely to be arrested and almost four times as likely to experience the use of force during encounters with the police.
3. **Students of color face harsher punishments in school than their white peers, leading to a higher number of youth of color incarcerated**. Black and Hispanic students represent more than 70 percent of those involved in school-related arrests or referrals to law enforcement. Currently, African Americans make up two-fifths and Hispanics one-fifth of confined youth today.
4. **According to recent data by the Department of Education, African American students are arrested far more often than their white classmates**. The data showed that 96,000 students were arrested and 242,000 referred to law enforcement by schools during the 2009-10 school year. Of those students, black and Hispanic students made up more than 70 percent of arrested or referred students. Harsh school punishments, from suspensions to arrests, have led to high numbers of youth of color coming into contact with the juvenile-justice system and at an earlier age.
5. **African American youth have higher rates of juvenile incarceration and are more likely to be sentenced to adult prison**. According to the Sentencing Project, even though African American juvenile youth are about 16 percent of the youth population, 37 percent of their cases are moved to criminal court and 58 percent of African American youth are sent to adult prisons.
6. **As the number of women incarcerated has increased by 800 percent over the last three decades, women of color have been disproportionately represented**. While the number of women incarcerated is relatively low, the racial and ethnic disparities are startling. African American women are three times more likely than white women to be incarcerated, while Hispanic women are 69 percent more likely than white women to be incarcerated.
7. **The war on drugs has been waged primarily in communities of color where people of color are more likely to receive higher offenses**. According to the Human Rights Watch, people of color are no more likely to use or sell illegal drugs than whites, but they have higher rate of arrests. African Americans comprise 14 percent of regular drug users but are 37 percent of those arrested for drug

offenses. From 1980 to 2007 about one in three of the 25.4 million adults arrested for drugs was African American.

8. **Once convicted, black offenders receive longer sentences compared to white offenders.** The U.S. Sentencing Commission stated that in the federal system black offenders receive sentences that are 10 percent longer than white offenders for the same crimes. The Sentencing Project reports that African Americans are 21 percent more likely to receive mandatory-minimum sentences than white defendants and are 20 percent more like to be sentenced to prison.

9. **Voter laws that prohibit people with felony convictions to vote disproportionately impact men of color.** An estimated 5.3 million Americans are denied the right to vote based on a past felony conviction. Felony disenfranchisement is exaggerated by racial disparities in the criminal-justice system, ultimately denying 13 percent of African American men the right to vote. Felony-disenfranchisement policies have led to 11 states denying the right to vote to more than 10 percent of their African American population.

10. **Studies have shown that people of color face disparities in wage trajectory following release from prison.** Evidence shows that spending time in prison affects wage trajectories with a disproportionate impact on black men and women. The results show no evidence of racial divergence in wages prior to incarceration; however, following release from prison, wages grow at a 21 percent slower rate for black former inmates compared to white ex-convicts. A number of states have bans on people with certain convictions working in domestic health-service industries such as nursing, child care, and home health care—areas in which many poor women and women of color are disproportionately concentrated.

Theses racial disparities have deprived people of color of their most basic civil rights, making criminal-justice reform the civil rights issue of our time. Through mass imprisonment and the overrepresentation of individuals of color within the criminal justice and prison system, people of color have experienced an adverse impact on themselves and on their communities from barriers to reintegrating into society to engaging in the democratic process. Eliminating the racial disparities inherent to our nation's criminal-justice policies and practices must be at the heart of a renewed, refocused, and reenergized movement for racial justice in America.

There have been a number of initiatives on the state and federal level to address the racial disparities in youth incarceration. Last summer Secretary of Education Arne Duncan announced the Schools Discipline Initiative to bring increased awareness of effective policies and practices to ultimately dismantle the school-to-prison pipeline. States like California and Massachusetts are considering legislation to address the disproportionate suspensions among students of color. And in Clayton County, Georgia, collaborative local reforms have resulted in a 47 percent reduction in juvenile-court referrals and a 51 percent decrease in juvenile felony rates. These initiatives could serve as models of success for lessening the disparities in incarceration rates.

CHAPTER 4

Unheard-of ways to achieve greater reading

Reading will increase your vocabulary, expand your understanding of the world around you, and it just might even be fun. If you run out of ideas, see Appendix A for 101 Recommended Books to Read. While 101 books might sound like a lot, it's really just a book a month from grades 7 to 12.

> *"Optimism is the faith that leads to achievement.*
>
> *Nothing can be done without hope and confidence."*
>
> – Helen Keller

Here are some more activities and ideas to boost your reading level.

Activity 1: Read the Newspaper

Whether it's online or a hard copy, read the newspaper (cover to cover, not just the comics or the sports) every day for a week. Read about the topics you're automatically interested in and the ones that are less appealing. If there's something that draws your attention, cut or print it out.

At the end of the week, ask yourself these questions: What have I learned?

- What new topics am I more interested in?
- How can I use this knowledge to boost my success in school?

Consider increasing your newspaper or news magazine reading. Current events knowledge is important in high school and college, and reading these periodicals gives you the chance to learn about a variety of topics from across the globe in a relatively short period of time.

Activity 2: Read a memoir

A memoir is a true story. Find one that appeals to you – maybe the story of someone who struggled in school, who didn't know what they wanted to be when they grew up or someone who had a lot of success in the things that you are interested in doing.

Read the book, not because you have to, but because you want to, from cover to cover. Sometimes reading about people's true lives is more fascinating and captivating than fiction.

Then, write your own one – to two-page memoir. It doesn't have to be a whole book to be worthwhile. Take what you learned about good memoir writing and put it to practice. Reading and writing go hand in hand – the better you are at one, the better you'll be at the other.

Read your memoir out loud to practice speaking – yet another skill that can help you in school!

Activity 3: Read everything you see

Read billboards. Read menus. Read signs at the bus stop. Read receipts.

For one week, practice paying attention to and reading everything you see that has writing on it.

For example, start reading:

- Ads
- Newsletters sent home from school
- The writing on the cereal box
- The small print
- Print on appliances, picture frames, and license plates
- Instructions
- Schedules

It doesn't matter what it is – just read it. We often get in the habit of glancing over things, especially familiar objects.

Notice if anything stands out or surprises you. Is there anything you want to read more or less of?

Read the world around you to increase your reading skills, your perception and your awareness of what's out there.

Summary

Reading is one of the best things you can do to boost your intelligence, your vocabulary, your writing skills and your educational success. Reading also allows you to explore other worlds, develop new ideas and gain different perspectives. Read anything you can get your hands on. Appendix A offers a variety of highly recommended books you can start reading!

Recommended for College-Bound Readers

It's a good idea to talk to your parents, librarians, teachers and counselors about your reading list. They can help you choose the best books for you from among your many options. Here are some suggestions to get you started.

Action Plan for Reading 200 Books in 12 Years

While 101 books might sound like a lot, it's really only one book a month from grade 7 through 12. You might read some of these in class, which will make them easy to check off the list, but you should cover the rest of the list on your own time.

Start by reading *Frankenstein*, *To Kill a Mockingbird*, *The Great Gatsby* and *Jane Eyre*. Continue with one book a month until you hit 101!

Author	Title
—	*Beowulf*
Achebe, Chinua	*Things Fall Apart*
Agee, James	*A Death in the Family*
Austen, Jane	*Pride and Prejudice*
Baldwin, James	*Go Tell It on the Mountain*
Beckett, Samuel	*Waiting for Godot*
Bellow, Saul	*The Adventures of Augie March*

Author	Title
Brontë, Charlotte	*Jane Eyre*
Brontë, Emily	*Wuthering Heights*
Camus, Albert	*The Stranger*
Cather, Willa	*Death Comes for the Archbishop*
Chaucer, Geoffrey	*The Canterbury Tales*
Chekhov, Anton	*The Cherry Orchard*
Chopin, Kate	*The Awakening*
Conrad, Joseph	*Heart of Darkness*
Cooper, James Fenimore	*The Last of the Mohicans*
Crane, Stephen	*The Red Badge of Courage*
Dante	*Inferno*
de Cervantes, Miguel	*Don Quixote*
Defoe, Daniel	*Robinson Crusoe*
Dickens, Charles	*A Tale of Two Cities*
Dostoyevsky, Fyodor	*Crime and Punishment*
Douglass, Frederick	*Narrative of the Life of Frederick Douglass*
Dreiser, Theodore	*An American Tragedy*
Dumas, Alexandre	*The Three Musketeers*
Eliot, George	*The Mill on the Floss*
Ellison, Ralph	*Invisible Man*
Emerson, Ralph Waldo	*Selected Essays*
Faulkner, William	*As I Lay Dying*
Faulkner, William	*The Sound and the Fury*
Fielding, Henry	*Tom Jones*
Fitzgerald, F. Scott	*The Great Gatsby*
Flaubert, Gustave	*Madame Bovary*
Ford, Ford Madox	*The Good Soldier*
Goethe, Johann Wolfgang von	*Faust*
Golding, William	*Lord of the Flies*
Hardy, Thomas	*Tess of the d'Urbervilles*
Hawthorne, Nathaniel	*The Scarlet Letter*
Heller, Joseph	*Catch-22*
Hemingway, Ernest	*A Farewell to Arms*
Homer	*The Iliad*
Homer	*The Odyssey*
Hugo, Victor	*The Hunchback of Notre Dame*

Author	Title
Hurston, Zora Neale	*Their Eyes Were Watching God*
Huxley, Aldous	*Brave New World*
Ibsen, Henrik	*A Doll's House*
James, Henry	*The Portrait of a Lady*
James, Henry	*The Turn of the Screw*
Joyce, James	*A Portrait of the Artist as a Young Man*
Kafka, Franz	*The Metamorphosis*
Kingston, Maxine Hong	*The Woman Warrior*
Lee, Harper	*To Kill a Mockingbird*
Lewis, Sinclair	*Babbitt*
London, Jack	*The Call of the Wild*
Mann, Thomas	*The Magic Mountain*
Marquez, Gabriel García	*One Hundred Years of Solitude*
Melville, Herman	*Bartleby the Scrivener*
Melville, Herman	*Moby Dick*
Miller, Arthur	*The Crucible*
Morrison, Toni	*Beloved*
O'Connor, Flannery	*A Good Man Is Hard to Find*
O'Neill, Eugene	*Long Day's Journey into Night*
Orwell, George	*Animal Farm*
Pasternak, Boris	*Doctor Zhivago*
Plath, Sylvia	*The Bell Jar*
Poe, Edgar Allan	*Selected Tales*
Proust, Marcel	*Swann's Way*
Pynchon, Thomas	*The Crying of Lot 49*
Remarque, Erich Maria	*All Quiet on the Western Front*
Rostand, Edmond	*Cyrano de Bergerac*
Roth, Henry	*Call It Sleep*
Salinger, J.D.	*The Catcher in the Rye*
Shakespeare, William	*Hamlet*
Shakespeare, William	*Macbeth*
Shakespeare, William	*A Midsummer Night's Dream*
Shakespeare, William	*Romeo and Juliet*
Shaw, George Bernard	*Pygmalion*
Shelley, Mary	*Frankenstein*
Silko, Leslie Marmon	*Ceremony*
Solzhenitsyn, Alexander	*One Day in the Life of Ivan Denisovich*

Spin a Soft Black Song by Nikki Giovanni

Black Boy by Richard Wright

Things Fall Apart by Chinua Achebe

Monster by Walter Dean Myers

When I Was The Greatest by Jason Reynolds

Miracle's Boys by Jacqueline Woodson

After Tupac and D Foster by Jacqueline Woodson

The Absolutely True Diary of a Part-Time Indian by Sherman Alexie

American Born Chinese by Gene Luen Yang

Crossover by Kwame Alexander

Quick Tip: Hey parents! Have your child read this book alongside a documentary on basketball. The National Common Core expects students to be able to, "Compare and contrast two or more characters, settings, or events in a story (or stories) or drama, drawing on specific details in the text (e.g., how characters interact)." CCSS.ELA-LITERACY.RL.5.3 Try Lebron James' "More Than A Game" or the classic "Hoop Dreams." Use the documentary/book in a discussion of comparing/contrasting. Have your child write a response to the film/book and feel free to give them a prompt that'll call on their comprehension and their interest.

11. The Color of Water by James McBride
12. The Autobiography of Malcolm X
13. Anansi Stories
14. The Alchemist by Paulo Coehlo
15. The Bluest Eye by Toni Morrison
16. All-American Boys by Brandon Kiely and Jason Reynolds
17. Kaffir Boy by Mark Mathabane
18. Dreams From My Father by Barack Obama
19. Bad Boy by Walter Dean Myers
20. Hoops by Walter Dean Myers
21. Buck by MK Asante

Quick Tip: Be sure to check the language/scenes/grade levels of books, before recommending them to your child. For intense texts, like "Buck" or Junot Diaz's "Drown", take into account the child/teen you're giving the book to. Is this a child that uses profanity? Is this a child that's seen/heard a lot of what's happening in the text? Could they benefit from reading something harsh and true to life, considering they might be living through it?

22. The Chocolate War by Robert Comier

23. The Best of Simple by Langston Hughes

24. Makes Me Wanna Holler by Nathan McCall

25. The Pact by Sampson Davis

26. The Bond by Sampson Davis

27. Invisible Man by Ralph Ellison

28. X by Ilyasah Shabazz

Quick Tip: X can be used as a "connector text." Get your child hype about Malcolm X's story, through this adventure and then introduce them to the autobiography.

29. The Boy In The Black Suit by Jason Reynolds

30. The Watsons go to Birmingham by Christopher Paul Curtis

31. Yolanda's Genius, by Carol Fenner

32. Esperanza Rising, by Pam Munoz Rising

33. The First Part Last, by Angela Johnson

34. March: Graphic Novels by John Lewis

35. Martin Luther King and The Montgomery Story

36. A Lesson Before Dying by Ernest Gaines

37. Roll of Thunder Hear My Cry by Mildred D. Taylor

38. Not Without Laughter by Langston Hughes

39. Marvel's New Black Panther Run by Ta-Nehisi Coates

39. 145th Street By Walter Dean Myers

40. Mexican White Boy By Matt De La Pena

41. Ball Don't Lie By Matt De La Pena

42. Game By Walter Dean Myers

43. Bang By Sharon G. Flake

44. You Don't Even Know Me by Sharon G. Flake

45. Tyrell By Coe Booth

46. Bronxwood By Coe Booth

47. Hip-Hop High School By Alan Larence Sitomer

48. Tears of a Tiger By Sharon M. Draper

49. Forged By Fire By Sharon M. Draper

50. Diary of Tears by Julius Lester

51. Elijah of Buxton by Christopher Paul Curtis

52. Bud Not Buddy by Christopher Paul Curtis

53. Sounder by William H. Armstrong

54. One Crazy Summer by Rita Williams-Garcia

55. Drown by Junot Diaz

56. The Beautiful Struggle by Ta-Nehisi Coates

57. The Dew Breaker by Edwidge Danticat

58. When the Beat Was Born: DJ Kool Herc and the Creation of Hip Hop by Laban Carrick Hill

59. Black Boy, White School by Brian F. Walker

60. Punished: Policing the Lives of Black and Latino Boys by Victor M. Rios

61. Letters to A Young Brother by Hill Harper

62. Barber Game Time Books by Tiki and Ronde Barber

63. Kid Caramel series by Dwayne Ferguson

64. The Toothpaste Millionaire by Jean Merrill

65. STAT: Standing Tall and Talented series by Amare Stoudemire

66. Miami Jackson series by Patricia McKissack

67. Julian series by Ann Cameron

68. Salt in His Shoes by Deloris Jordan

69. Be Boy Buzz by bell hooks

70. Between The World and Me by Ta-Nehisi Coates

71. Shooting Kabul by N.H. Senzai

72. 12 Years A Slave: Illustrated Edition

73. I Never Had It Made: an Autobiography of Jackie Robinson

74. Pull by Kevin Waltman

75. Kinda Like Brothers by Coe Booth

76. Dopesick by Walter Dean Myers

77. Lockdown by Walter Dean Myers

78. All The Right Stuff by Walter Dean Myers
79. Darius & Twig by Walter Dean Myers
80. How It Went Down by Kekla Magoon
81. Blue Boy by Rakesh Satyal
82. Yummy: The Last Days of a Southside Shorty by G. Neri
83. Ghetto Cowboy by G. Neri
84. Boys Without Names by Kashmira Steth
85. Chess Rumble by G. Neri
86. Keeping the Night Watch by Hope Anita Smith
87. He Said, She Said by Kwame Alexander
88. Turning 15 On the Road to Freedom by Elspeth Lealock
89. A Wreath for Emmit Till by Marilyn Johnson
90. Mississippi Trial, 1955 by Chris Crowe
91. The Battle of Jericho by Sharon M. Draper
92. We Beat The Street by Sampson Davis
93. Superman Vs. Muhammad Ali by Neal Adams/Dennis O'Neil
94. Spiderman: Miles Morales
95. Life Doesn't Frighten Me by Maya Angelou & Jean-Michel Basquiat
96. It's Bigger Than Hip-Hop by MK Asante
97. Can't Stop, Won't Stop by Jeff Chang
98. As Brave As You by Jason Reynolds
99. Ghost by Jason Reynolds
100. Jaden Toussaint, The Greatest by Marti Dumas

Tips for Making the Transition to College

Improving your literacy level is just one of the many ways you can better prepare yourself to go from high school to college. As we've discussed, reading is an essential skill that boosts your intelligence, expands your vocabulary, and increases your understanding of the world around you. Having more advanced reading skills is essential if you are to be successful in college, because the amount of reading that will be required of you will be significantly more than what you had to do in high school. The complexity of the readings in college is also much more difficult than high school readings. But there are many other areas that you can improve upon to ensure you have the best shot at success in college.[29]

Don't Miss Orientation

Orientation is your first chance to get an in-depth look at your new school. It's also a great time to meet new people and forge friendships. Usually, orientation will involve a number of activities, including activities to get to know other students, introductions to professors, and a tour of campus.

> *"Let it [racism] be a problem to someone else... Let it drag them down. Don't use it as an excuse for your own shortcomings."*
> – Colin Powell

Getting familiar with all these aspects of college before classes begin is essential for you to feel as comfortable as possible that first day of class. Missing out on meeting new people or finding where your classes will be can cause you a lot of unneeded stress as you begin your college

---

[29] "Transitioning From High School to College Academics," College View, accessed 21 Jan 2015, http://www.collegeview.com/articles/article/transitioning-from-high-school-to-college-academics.

career, so make every effort to take part in as many orientation activities as you can!

Go to Class

It might seem obvious that you need to go to class in order to be a successful college student. However, many kids have gone to college and failed miserably because they didn't go to class. Professors don't take attendance. If you miss a class, you aren't going to get detention like you did in high school

If you go away to college, your mom, dad, aunt, or brother won't be there to wake you up. You have to develop the self-control to get enough sleep so you can get out of bed and get to class on time, every single day.

Showing up to class is the only way you will stay on top of what's going on, and is the only way you can determine what your professor thinks is important for you to learn. You also can't take notes or ask questions in a class you don't attend. Since many tests in college are based upon lectures and inclass activities, it's especially important that you attend class on a regular basis.

Study, Study, Study

The pace of learning in college is faster, the material is more in-depth, and the expectations of you are much higher than they were in high school. All of that translates into you spending more time hitting the books and less time at parties or hanging out with friends. This is true for students who had trouble making it through high school as well as for those that breezed right through to graduation.

Over time, you will develop time management skills that will allow you to study more efficiently and regain some free time. But initially, maybe even for the first semester or entire first year you are in college, you won't have all the freedom and free time that you might have thought you would have. Although college should be a fun experience, the purpose is to get your degree! Studying is a central component of you getting your college degree so you can get a good job and lead a good life.

There are lots of ways that you can get yourself into the routine of getting sufficient study time every day. Whether you live in the dorms or at home with your family, you may not have the quiet and privacy you need to get your work done. A simple solution is to allot some time each day to study in the library at your college. There will be plenty of tables, cubicles, and quiet corners in the library where you can study in peace.

Scheduling is also a big part of studying. If possible, block out a consistent time each day for doing your homework. Maybe that's during lunch, after your last class, or before you go to bed. But choosing a time that is consistent will establish a routine that your body and mind can get used to. A helpful tip is to study during the time of day when you are most alert and have the most energy. If that means you study from midnight to 2:00 am, do it so long as it doesn't interfere with your class schedule.

It's also hard to study if you aren't organized. In high school, it's easier to stay on top of assignments because your teachers and parents likely reminded you of due dates and upcoming tests. In college, that responsibility rests squarely on your shoulders. Get in the habit of writing down when assignments are due or when tests are coming up. You can do this in a planner or calendar, or use the calendar app on your phone to set reminders. Also strive to keep your books, notebooks, and binders organized and orderly. Have a dedicated notebook and folder for each class, so assignments from your math class don't end up with your assignments from English. Nothing says, "I'm unprepared for college" to your professors like a student that loses his or her homework. Don't be that guy!

Utilize Campus Resources

To keep yourself on the right track in college, it's important for you to take advantage of the resources available to you. Your professors will be one of the greatest resources you can have while you're in college. Professors will maintain office hours, which is a period of time each day that they are available to meet with students. If you ever have questions about anything in your classes, schedule an appointment to meet with your professor immediately. While it can be a bit intimidating to ask for help, professors are there for YOUR benefit

It is their job to help you learn and grow, and they can't do that job if they don't know you're struggling with something. Even if you're doing great in class, it's always a good idea to meet with your professor periodically. This will help you form a more personal bond with your professors and will demonstrate to them that you are committed to learning and committed to their class.

> *"The battles that count aren't the ones for gold medals.*
>
> *The struggles within yourself-the invisible, inevitable battles inside all of us-that's where it's at."*
>
> – Jesse Owens

Colleges all have tutoring and academic assistance programs designed to help students that need a little extra help in order to be successful. Many students don't seek help out of pride, but if you find that you're getting behind or that you don't understand the concepts you're studying, swallowing your pride and asking for help is the right thing to do. Oftentimes, academic assistance programs will be staffed by other students, so you can get help from someone that has already taken the class that is causing you struggles.

Another great resource is your academic advisor. When you go to college you will have an advisor that will work with you on creating your schedule, checking to make sure you're progressing on your credits, ensure that you're meeting graduation requirements, and help you identify areas that are weak or lacking that you need to address. They will be able to provide information about certain professors as well. For example, if you are a visual learner, they may be able to tell you which professors utilize visual learning methods. Academic advisors are also responsible for confronting you if your grades aren't where they should be and may get you involved in tutoring or other support services if your grades slip.

College can be an incredibly stressful period in your life, so taking advantage of on-campus programs to help you deal with that stress is a good idea. Colleges and universities have campus life programs that include fun activities for students to help them keep from feeling overwhelmed. While your focus should be on your studies, getting good grades, and graduating, you also need to have some time set aside to enjoy your college experience. Attend sporting events, go to concerts, or join a club. Going to an event on campus will help you wind down, have fun, and let some of the stress and pressure from school melt away.

Sometimes, college students need more than just fun out with friends in order to deal with personal issues that come up during college. About 27% of college students have depression, another 24% have bipolar disorder, and 11% have anxiety.[30] Since so many students have mental health concerns, colleges and universities have counseling centers, where students can meet with a counselor to discuss any problems they are having that are impacting their mood, emotions, or school performance. These services are usually offered for free to students, so getting the help you need to be mentally strong is just a matter of making an appointment and talking to a professional.

Make Your Schedule Work for You

When you're in college, you get to choose what classes to take, when to take them, and what professor teaches your classes. As a freshman, you will get the last draw when it comes to classes, so you won't always get what you want. However, you should strive to build a class schedule that sets you up for success. This involves a few considerations:

- Spread out difficult classes. If you struggle in math, don't take two math classes in one semester. At the same time, don't take a bunch of "cake" courses that are really easy all in one semester. Come up with a good balance so you have some easier classes and harder classes each semester.
- Schedule classes for optimal times of the day. If you're a morning person, try to get as many morning classes as possible. If you're a night owl, think about taking some evening courses. Be purposeful about what classes you take and when so you can capitalize on your brainpower and your body's energy level.
- Meet with your academic advisor to make sure that the classes you want to take are the classes you need to graduate. Although you will need to take some general classes and elective courses, you don't want

---

[30] "College Students Speak: A Survey Report on Mental Health," National Alliance on Mental Illness, 2012, accessed 22 Jan 2015, http://www.nami.org/Content/NavigationMenu/Find_Support/NAMI_on_Campus1/NAMI_Survey_on_College_Students/collegereport.pdf.

to spend your time and money on classes that won't count towards your degree.

Get Involved

Part of the college experience is getting involved in activities with your peers. This is especially important if you live off campus so that you can make connections with your classmates. Colleges and universities have many clubs and organizations for students to join, from fraternities and sororities to service oriented clubs to honor societies. There are also many options for staying active, with many campuses offering club team sports, adventure outings, and informal games like flag football or ultimate Frisbee. Having outlets for fun will help you manage the stress associated with college and will also help you bond with other students at your school.

Conclusion

Unlike K-12 public school, college is optional. There is no law that says you have a right to get a college education. Viewing college as a privilege will help you keep your focus on studying and getting good grades. Remember, college is your ticket to a much better life! A lot of college students end up dropping out because they can't make the transition from being a high school kid with a lot of adult support, to being an adult responsible for his or her own actions. If you follow the tips in this chapter and make responsible decisions while also having some fun along the way, you will have a successful college career.

CHAPTER 5

Professional Athletics is Not Your Ticket to Success

Many young men dream of someday playing professional athletics and being the next LeBron James, Kevin Durant, Russell Wilson or Dez Bryant. It may be even more enticing to dream of being a professional athlete when superstars like LeBron, who never went to college, or Kevin, who left college after one year, have gone on to be among the best athletes of our time, while making a whole lot of money doing it. While it's good to have lofty goals and set high expectations for yourself, making it as a pro athlete is much, much more difficult – and rare – than it seems, especially for athletes that don't go to college.

> *"Keep your eyes on the stars, and your feet on the ground."*
> – Theodore Roosevelt

There are a few numbers you should consider to understand better just how hard it is to become a college athlete, let alone become a pro:[31]

- In 2013, there were about 540,000 high school boys that played basketball. Of those, less than 18,000 played basketball in college. Just 46 college basketball players were drafted that year. Only 3.3% of high school students went on to play at college, and just 1.2% of college basketball players went on to play at the professional level. Only 0.03% of high school basketball players went on to be drafted professionally.

---

[31] "Probability of Competing Beyond High School," National Collegiate Athletics Association, 2013, accessed 25 Jan 2015, http://www.ncaa.org/about/resources/research/probability-competing-beyond-high-school.

- In 2013, nearly 1.1 million high school boys played football. Of those, just over 70,000 became NCAA student-athletes. There were 254 college football players drafted that year. This means that just 6.5% of high school football players made it to play in college while just 1.6% of college football players ended up being drafted by a professional team. A mere 0.08% of high school football players were drafted.
- There were only 460,000 NCAA student-athletes in 2013. That's less than the number boys that played high school baseball that year.
- The 460,000 NCAA student-athlete figure is the total for men and women at every college in the United States. Only 2% of them will ever play professional sports.

These figures aren't presented to you in order to rain on your parade. Being involved in athletics in high school is an excellent choice because it gives you an opportunity to learn and grow outside of the classroom, gain valuable personal skills, and improve your communication, teamwork, and time-management skills. Additionally, sports help you develop an excellent work ethic, keeps you healthy, and keeps you safe and off the streets. And for some high school athletes, their physical skills get them scholarships to college. There's a lot of good things about sports, but you shouldn't view them as your ticket to success because it is so rare that sports gets you to the next level, whether that's in college or on a professional team.

Instead, your ticket to success is education. Going to college should be your primary goal when you think about your life and your future after high school. Although some high school kids think that they don't have what it takes to get into college, this is not the case. In 2013, almost 66% of high school graduates enrolled in college.[32] While some schools, like Harvard, Yale, and Stanford, have extremely competitive admissions with fewer than 20% of applicants accepted, other schools like community colleges, technical colleges, and state universities have much higher rates of acceptance. In fact, some schools, particularly community colleges, have what's called open enrollment, which means that anyone that graduates from high school or has their G.E.D. is accepted.[33] Even if you don't have the best grades, or you struggle in a

---

[32] "College Enrollment and Work Activity of 2013 High School Graduates," Bureau of Labor Statistics, 2014, accessed on 25 Jan 2015, http://www.bls.gov/news.release/hsgec.nr0.htm.

[33] "What Students Need to Know About Community Colleges," College Board, 2015, accessed 25 Jan 2015, http://professionals.collegeboard.com/guidance/college/community-college.

particular subject, you can still get into college, get a degree, and improve your chances for a bright future.

So when thinking about your future and the possibilities for success, you need to play the odds. Do you put your money on pursuing a career as a professional athlete, which less than one-half of one percent of high school kids achieves? Or do you put your money on going to college, which if you graduate from high school or have a G.E.D. is virtually guaranteed? The choice seems clear!

> *"Success is to be measured not so much by the position that one has reached in life as by the obstacles which he has overcome while trying to succeed."*
> – Booker T. Washington

In this chapter, you will explore a few topics related to learning, including learning styles, tips for improving your learning, and strategies for taking notes and studying for tests. Use the information in this chapter to improve your achievement at school. Remember, it is through education, not professional sports, that you will be able to punch your ticket to a brighter future!

Learn Something New Every Day

The smartest and most successful people in life are always growing and always learning. With that in mind, take it upon yourself to learn something new every single day. This should be pretty easy if you're showing up to class regularly!

Learning something new might be a new word in English, a new fact in biology or a new and improved way of interacting with your teachers or classmates. Write down what you learn every day and look back at it periodically – you might be impressed by how much new knowledge you gain with your good attendance and desire to learn more. If something really excites you, consider learning even more about it or basing a class project on your favorite new topic. Never stop learning!

How many of you study more than 2 hours a night? How many study less? Who worries about tests? If your teacher announced a surprise test today, how many of you would be prepared right now? How many would like to have more free time to do fun things and still get good grades? Sounds great doesn't it? This is something you can achieve because there are ways to improve how to study by learning about your specific learning style and learning test-taking strategies. You CAN have time for that fun stuff and definitely improve your grades in high school and beyond if you decide to continue your education.

Virtually all learning is based on memory. The more you remember, the better grades you'll get. It's simply a matter of utilizing the learning style that works for you. Then, it's easy to get the results you want: clearer thinking, better grades, higher self-esteem, and even down the road, a better career and more money.

What is a 'learning style'? Any ideas? Learning styles are various ways of learning. Have you ever noticed that in order for some people to learn something, they have to read it or say it out loud? Others, though, could read a paragraph six times without learning anything, but if you give them a hands-on project they'll never forget it. Still others need to hear things in order to learn the best.

There are basically three ways people learn, and it is important to understand which learning style best suits you in order to capitalize on your strengths and improve on your weaknesses.

Visual – about 60% of people are visual learners. It helps to see their teacher's body language and they are assisted greatly by the use of diagrams, handouts, and illustrations. It is often best for visual learners to sit in the front of the classroom where there are fewer distractions. Visual learners usually benefit from taking detailed notes as this helps them absorb the information further. If a visual learner is asked to spell a word, they usually have to write it down to make sure it's correct. If you can "picture" things in your mind very easily, you are likely a visual learner. About 60% of all people have a visual learning style and are the fastest learners.

Auditory – 25% of people learn best by hearing. Discussions and lectures from the teacher really appeal to auditory learners. They tend to focus on the speaker's voice tone, pitch, speed and other nuances of speech. Written information doesn't have much meaning until it has been spoken and heard, so notes are normally not helpful for auditory. Auditory learners can usually pick up songs and foreign languages fairly quickly.

Kinesthetic – if you learn through moving, doing, and touching you are a kinesthetic learner. About 15% of all people fall into this category. Also called tactile learners, kinesthetic people need the hands-on approach. Touching things, trying them out, and moving around while discussing an issue are all ways to actively explore the subject at hand and discover its meaning. This is why some kids may have a hard time sitting still for long periods of time and simply listening to lecture. Kinesthetic learners are likely to relate experiences with strong feelings and know they have truly grasped something once they feel it inside. Great athletes are usually kinesthetic learners.

Your learning style determines how you digest information. In school, you are more likely to comprehend information if you can translate it into the language that your body and mind naturally understand. Different people learn in different ways and knowing your preferred style is one of the keys to improving your grades!

So, you understand that identifying your learning style is important. But how do you do it? The first step is to take a test of some sort that will help you determine the learning style you rely on the most. You can take a personality test, such as the Meyers-Briggs test, or you can take a test that is focused on just learning styles. You may want to see your teacher or guidance counselor about taking a test like this

Real Talk

Five Letters

That Can Really Affect Your Life

Grades can affect career options, earning potential and self-image. Almost everyone has the mental ability to get better grades, or to get those A's with less stress. It's a matter of believing in yourself and desiring to do well. No matter what kind of grades you get, A's, B's, C's, D's, or F's there's a way to increase your learning potential, to do it smarter and take less time doing it. Henry Ford summed it all up when he said, "If you think you can do well, you're right. If you think you can't do well, you're right." You hold the key to your own success.

What are some ways, beginning right now, that you can improve your ability to get better grades and make learning more enjoyable? Do you have any ideas? Listening, reading, note-taking, memorization, and time management are all good answers.

6 Steps to Better Grades

- ☐ Attendance
- ☐ Listening – TLQR
- ☐ Reading
- ☐ Note-taking – Cornell System
- ☐ Memorization
- ☐ Time Management

Let's start working smarter by discussing the easiest improvement first:

1. Attendance: Does anyone know how to average 80% on tests without cracking a book? Be in class. Studies have shown that roughly 80% of test material is given orally in class by the teacher. So, if you have a test every four weeks and you miss two of those days, you have potentially lowered your test grade by 10%.

2. Listening: Listening is another way to learn faster. But, it's like driving a car without brakes since you can think four times faster than someone can talk. This leaves a lot of time for daydreaming.

> *"I believe in the brotherhood of man, all men, but I don't believe in brotherhood with anybody who doesn't want brotherhood with me. I believe in treating people right, but I'm not going to waste my time trying to treat somebody right who doesn't know how to return the treatment."*
>
> – Malcolm X

One key to good listening is to use the TLQR process:

- ☐ **Tune In.** Right as the lecture begins, determine the topic, and recall what you may already know about the topic.

- **Question.** Early in the lecture, continue the listening process by asking questions in your mind such as: "What point is the teacher making?" "What devices for support is he/she using?" "What do I need to remember specifically?"
- **Listen.** This part of the process includes determining the basic message and answering the questions being raised during the total process. In order to accomplish this, you must anticipate what will be said, and take in what is said. Active alertness is ALWAYS REQUIRED.
- **Review.** This is the process of checking on the anticipated message after the message is delivered. To review, you must evaluate the message against your questions. Fit ideas together, summarize ideas and evaluate the meaning and impact of the message. This review process should lead to further questions and keep you constantly tuned into the lecture.

3. Reading: Reading puts a wealth of information at your fingertips. The more you read, the more you learn. The main key to faster reading is the proper use of your hands as it establishes a faster pace, enhances concentration, and prevents regression, or re-reading by accident. The dominant hand becomes the reading hand. Use your fingertips to glide across the page under the words being read and to lead your eyes back to the next line. The opposite hand is for page turning and will be curled above the book with the thumb, index, and middle finger anticipating page turns. Practicing this technique can actually get you up to almost 900 words per minute, instead of the average of 250. Speeds will vary with the nature of the material and your familiarity with it. Obviously, complex technical material requires more concentration and detail. With literature, you may uncover the plot and perceive the emotions, but you won't truly experience the emotions by speedreading. If you have difficulty understanding what you have read, misunderstanding faster doesn't help you!

4. Note-Taking: There are several methods used for note-taking. Forty years ago, Walter Pauk developed what is known as the **Cornell note-taking technique** to help Cornell University students better organize their notes. This is the most popular note-taking strategy in the United States.

Pauk Outlines Six Steps in the Cornell Note-taking system:

1. Record
(During Lecture)
• Write down facts and ideas in phrases
• Use abbreviations when poss.
(After Lecture)
• Read through your notes
• Fill in blanks and make scribbles more legible
2. Reduce or Question
(After Lecture)
• Write keywords, phrases or questions that serve as cues for notes taken in class
• Cue phrases and questions should be in your own words
3. Recite
• With classroom notes covered, read each keyword or question
• Recite the fact or idea brought to mind by the keyword or question
4. & 5. Reflect and Review
• Review your notes periodically by reciting
• Think about what you have learned
6. Recapitulation (After Lecture)
• Summarize each main idea
• Use complete sentences

To begin with Cornell notes, divide your notepaper into three sections. At the bottom, create a two-inch tall box that extends the width of the paper. Above that, create two columns, one on the left that is one-third the width of the sheet and the other on the right that is two-thirds the width of the sheet.

- Record: Simply record as many facts and ideas as you can in the right column. Don't be concerned with getting everything or writing your notes grammatically correct. Try leaving out unnecessary words and using only key verbs. To ensure notes make sense later on, after the lecture is over fill in blanks or make incomplete sentences complete.

- Reduce or question: After you read through your notes, your next step is to reduce important facts and ideas to keywords or phrases or to formulate questions based on the facts and ideas. These keywords, phrases, and questions are written in the narrow column on the left side of the paper. These words and phrases act as memory cues so that when you review them, you will recall the ideas or facts. The questions help to clarify the meanings of the facts and ideas.

- Recite: Recitation is a very powerful process in the retention of information. Reciting is different from re-reading in that you state out loud and in your own words the facts and ideas that you are trying to learn. It is an effective way to learn because hearing your thoughts helps you to sharpen your thinking process. Stating ideas and facts in your own words challenges you to think about the meaning of the information. When reciting, cover up your notes in the right-hand column, while leaving the cue words and questions uncovered and readily accessible.

- Reflect: Reflection is pondering or thinking about the information you have learned. Reflecting is a step beyond learning the content of your notes. It reinforces deeper learning by relating facts and ideas to other learning and knowledge. Questions to ask yourself: How do these facts and ideas fit into what I already know? How can I apply these facts? How is knowing this important? What is the significance of these facts and ideas?

- Review: The way to prevent forgetting is to review your notes frequently. Brief review sessions planned throughout the term, perhaps weekly, will aid more complete comprehension and retention of information than will cramming the day before a test. It will cut down on stress too!

- Recapitulate: The recapitulation or summary of your notes goes at the bottom of the note page in the two-inch block. Taking a few minutes after you have reduced, recited, and reflected to

> "I don't want a Black History Month. Black history is American history."
> – Morgan Freeman

summarize the facts and ideas in your notes will help you integrate the information. The summary should not be a word-for-word rewriting of your notes. It should be in your own words and reflect the main points you want to remember from your notes. Reading through your summaries in preparation for an exam is a great way to review to **increase your grades**!

The Cornell System was designed for lecture note-taking, but fits easily in taking notes while reading from a textbook. Its greatest benefit will be to aid in the recall process.

This brings us to our next part:

5. Memorization. For quizzes and tests, you'll be required to memorize lists of names or items. Who likes to memorize? One easy way to retain information is to use tricks like word associations, substitutions, acronyms, and visualization. Do you remember the acronym for the names of the Great Lakes? H.O.M.E.S. Can you name them? (Recite: Huron, Ontario, Michigan, Erie, and Superior). But an acronym only works if you remember it. One method is the link system. The link system is used to remember things in sequence. Take each word and visualize a ridiculous picture, then link the pictures together into a larger picture. The more bizarre and exaggerated, the better.

Here is an example: Using the link system you can remember ten totally unrelated words, like **airplane, trees, envelopes, earring, bucket, pizza, star, nose, singing, and basketball**. The trick to remember all ten words is to visualize an airplane and a long line of giant trees boarding the airplane. Each tree is carrying an envelope. Earrings are hanging from the envelopes. Each tree drops his envelope into a bucket as he boards. There is a huge pizza in the bucket with a star on it. Each tree sniffs the pizza with his nose as he boards the airplane. Inside the airplane, the trees are singing and playing basketball. Now, without looking at the list, see how many words you can remember. How many did you get? If you really see these pictures in your mind, you won't be able to forget these ten words. In fact, you'll be able to recite them backwards! The mind never thinks without a mental picture. You can remember any new piece of information if it is associated with something else you already know. But, all these tricks won't do you any good if you don't have the time to utilize them.

6. Time Management. You have probably heard the phrase "Time is money". Do you know what that means? One of the toughest skills to master is time management. Some days do you feel like there is just too much to do and not enough time to do it? You have so many competing demands on your time: school, friends, homework, family, sports, movies and on and on. How can you come to grips with all of it? You might wish for more time, but may not realize you are the only one who can create it. Most time management experts say that one of the first things you need to do to manage your time is to determine how you spend your time in the first place. If you take a good look at how you currently spend each 24 hours, you might find that there are things you can do to make better use of this time. Time management is all about managing yourself!

You cannot spend all your time wisely – nor should you. But you shouldn't waste all your time either. You need to learn how to balance the time you spend on wise and unwise activities. Becoming aware of how you spend your time now is the first step in planning how to spend your time in the future. One way is to make a Daily Activity Log – a listing of activities you do from the time you get up until the time you go to sleep – to see how you spend your time. There is a daily activity log at the end of this chapter for you to use to track your time.

Daily Activity Log

There are several ways to make sure you can have more time in a day. The first way to gain more time is to plan it! It's like getting in a car and going somewhere. If you know where you're going and have a plan to get there, such as a road map, then you will get there without wasting time. If you do not have a plan, then you will be wasting time and will take longer to get to your destination, if you get there at all!

A second way to gain more time in a day is to do more in less time. This can be as simple as doubling up on activities. For example, if you have three errands to do on your way home from school, instead of doing one at a time, you may be able to combine them and make one round-trip instead of three. If you commute on a bus or ride with friends or family, you could study on your way to school or work. While eating lunch, you could review your notes.

The third way to gain more time is to use short periods of otherwise wasted time. Do you have a free half hour between classes where you can either socialize with friends or study? If **doing well in school is important to you**, you might choose to study sometimes instead of socializing. Do you watch a lot of T.V. or constantly talk on the phone? Try reducing or limiting these activities and incorporating more time for your studies. Furthermore, it's not a bad idea to carry some of your study material or homework with you because you never know when you will have to wait for something or someone. If each day (Monday through Friday) you found an extra 30 minutes of study time, in one week you would have an extra 2 ½ hours!

There are only twenty-four hours in a day, no more, no less. To spend it wisely means you are spending it productively toward a goal. To spend it unwisely means you are wasting time. If you put off an assignment for too long, you may not get it done on time. The assignment also may not be a quality job or as complete as the teacher desires. Difficult assignments do not get any easier when they are put off.

Up to this point we have discussed several methods for you to improve your grades. Now think about the day of the test. Examinations are a fact of life in high school and college. If you take a multiple-choice exam your strategy will be different than if you were to take an essay test. One sign that you aren't prepared is when you have to stay up all night to "cram". Cramming won't do very much for you (except make you so tired that when you take the exam you won't be able to think clearly enough to answer the questions you DO know).

What follows are some test-taking tips that will help you succeed in your quest for excellence in school.

Test-Taking Strategies

Before You Begin:

Preview the test before you answer anything. This gets you thinking about the material. Make sure to note the point value of each question. This will give you some ideas on budgeting your time.

Do a mind dump. Using what you saw in the preview, make notes of anything you think you might forget. Write down things that you used in learning the material that might help you remember. Outline your answers to discussion questions.

Quickly calculate how much time you should allow for each section according to the point value. You don't want to spend 30 minutes on an essay question that counts for only 5 points and just 10 minutes on a multiple choice section worth 25 points.

Taking the Test:

- *Read the directions.* Can more than one answer be correct? Are you penalized for guessing? Never assume that you know what the directions will say.
- *Answer the easy questions first.* This will give you the confidence and momentum to get through the rest of the test. It will also ensure that you've answered as many questions as possible in case you run out of time.
- *Go back to the difficult questions.* While looking over the test and doing the easy questions, your subconscious mind will have been working on the answers to the harder ones. Also, later items on the test might give you useful or needed information to answer earlier items.
- *Answer all questions.* Unless you are penalized for incorrect responses or guessing, always put an answer for every question.
- *Ask the instructor to explain any items that are not clear.* Your teacher is there to help, so don't be afraid to ask for clarification on confusing questions.
- *Try to answer the questions from the instructor's point of view.* Try to remember what the instructor emphasized in class as to what they felt was most important.
- *Use the margin to explain why you chose the answer.* If the question does not seem clear or if the answer seems ambiguous, write a quick note to explain why you chose the answer that you did. You might get some credit for

> *"We should emphasize not Negro History, but the Negro in history.*
>
> *What we need is not a history of selected races or nations, but the history of the world void of national bias, race hate, and religious prejudice."*
>
> – Carter Woodson

the answer if you can demonstrate how and why you thought about the question the way you did.
- *Circle keywords to difficult questions.* This will force you to focus on the central point.
- *Keep an eye on the clock and use all the time allotted for the test.* Review the exam and make sure you haven't left out any answers or parts or answers. Don't rush to be the first one done with the test!

Guidelines for Answering True-False Questions

1. When you don't know the answer, mark it true!
- Generally speaking, there are more questions whose answers are true.
- Instructors find it more difficult to create questions with answers that are false.
- If the question includes specific details, that may also be a good indication that the answer is true.

2. Look for any factor that will make a statement false.

3. Look for extreme modifiers in the question. Extreme modifiers such as always, all, never, or only are usually good indicators that the answer is false.

4. Qualifying words tend to make a question true. Qualifiers (seldom, often, many) increase the likelihood that the statement is true.

5. Questions that state a reason tend to be false. Words in the statement that cause justification or reason, such as since, because, when, or if, generally make the statement false. Also pay close attention to the reason that is given, because if it is incomplete the answer is likely false.

There is no substitute for the truth. Many concentrated hours of studying to force facts into your memory is the best way to prepare for true-false questions

Guidelines for Answering Multiple-choice Questions:

1. Try to formulate your own answer before reading the options given to you. If what you came up with on your own is one of the options, chances are it's the correct answer.

2. Eliminate unlikely answers first.

3. Select numbered answers from the middle range, not the extremes. For example, if the height of a mountain is requested, eliminate 20,000 feet (high) and 3,000 feet (low), and then choose between 8,000 feet and 11,000 feet.

4. Select answers that are longer and more descriptive.

5. Similar answers give you a clue! If two of the four possible answers are similar, one of them is correct, the other is disguised.

Guidelines for Answering Matching Questions:

1. Examine both lists to determine the types of items and their relationships.

2. Use one list as a starting point and go through the second list to find a match.

3. Move through the entire list before selecting a match because a more correct answer may follow.

4. Cross off items on the second list when you are certain that you have a match.

> *"Defining myself, as opposed to being defined by others, is one of the most difficult challenges I face."*
> – Carol Moseley-Braun

5. Do not guess until all absolute matches have been made. You will likely eliminate an answer that could be used for a later choice.

Guidelines for Essay Questions:

1. Organize your thoughts before you begin to write.

2. Paraphrase the original question to form your introductory statement. This process helps you get the question straight in your mind and helps structure your answer to address the question appropriately.

3. Use the principles of English composition. Form a clear statement of purpose and place it as near to the beginning as possible. Provide clear

explanations to back up the main concept. Remember, a complete answer usually has a main idea, supporting details and illustrative examples.

4. Write clearly! Teachers need to be able to read and understand your answer.

5. Use lists or bullets whenever possible in order to provide evidence to support your point.

After the Test:

If the teacher reviews the exam in class, make sure you pay attention. This helps reinforce the information one more time in long-term memory. Even if you aren't interested in the "learning" aspect of the class, it is an opportunity to hear what the teacher was looking for in the answers, which can help you on future tests because you will have a better idea of what to study.

In Closing

Your learning style, proper note-taking, time management, and test-taking strategies are all a vital part of improving your grade and your academic success. Everyone is capable of doing great things by eliminating poor habits and adding a few good ones. By mastering a smarter way to learn and saving time as well, you will gain a feeling of accomplishment, a feeling of success, and as your confidence grows, everything will seem less overwhelming. It's all in your hands – be the gardener – grow some healthy grades!

Daily Activity Log

6:00 _____	3:30 _____
6:30 _____	4:00 _____
7:30 _____	4:30 _____
8:00 _____	5:00 _____
8:30 _____	5:30 _____
9:00 _____	6:00 _____
9:30 _____	6:30 _____
10:00 _____	7:00 _____
10:30 _____	7:30 _____
11:00 _____	8:00 _____
11:30 _____	8:30 _____
12:00 _____	9:00 _____
12:30 _____	9:30 _____
1:00 _____	10:00 _____
1:30 _____	10:30 _____
2:00 _____	11:00 _____
2:30 _____	11:30 _____
3:00 _____	12:00 _____

How much time did you spend sleeping?

How much time did you spend eating & grooming?

How much time did you spend commuting?

How much time did you spend attending classes?

How much time did you spend working at a job?

How much time did you spend in sports or leisure activities?

How much time did you spend socializing with friends?

How much time did you spend watching TV?

How much time is not accounted for? (no activity listed)

What else did you spend your time doing?

CHAPTER 6

Why you need a change in your environment

Separating Friends from Responsibilities

Danny was one of those insanely popular jocks in high school, and when he went to college, the same sort of aura followed him there. He was very nice as well as smart, and this made a lot of different people like him. When he first got to college, many of the kids were partying and having a good time being away from home. Every night it seemed as if he was invited to another party, and he really didn't want to hurt anyone's feelings and not show up. For a little while, he was able to keep up with training sessions, studies, and assignments but after a while, the lack of sleep and the strain on his time began to take a toll. He got a terrible grade on something that he should have been able to pass in his sleep, and he was really upset. His basketball coach put him on probation, and he wasn't allowed to play any more games.

When he spoke to his coach about it, Danny got some great advice. His coach told Danny that he'd noticed the strain on Danny's time and alertness. He explained that things were completely different in college and while having a social life is okay, there is a real importance to separate your friends from your responsibilities. He also told him

> "What you get by achieving your goals is not as important as what you become by achieving your goals."
> – Henry David Thoreau

about maintaining an optimal performance level by resting and taking care of his body.

Danny thought this over for a while and understood that there was no way he could keep getting terrible grades. He also had to eat healthier and get regular sleep. After a while, he came up with a few compromises that helped him separate his social life from his responsibilities.

The first thing Danny did was schedule out parts of his day in hour-long blocks. After classes and basketball practice, he dedicated the first four hours to studying and completing homework. Then he allowed a free hour. During this hour, he could spend extra time playing basketball, studying for something particularly hard or he could reserve it for rest, calling home or anything else. After this, he dedicated the next few hours to being with his friends or visiting people and anything else that had to do with his social life.

Around 10pm, he was scheduled to be back in his dorm, and getting ready for another hour of study before it was time to hit the sack. By the next quarter, his grades improved significantly, and his coach allowed him back on the team.

His coach had noticed how Danny had straightened things out and seemed more alert and refreshed. He also realized that Danny's grades weren't dipping, and he appeared to be handling his social life rather well. Although Danny had a hard time in the beginning, he learned that by creating a tough schedule and sticking to it no matter what, he could accomplish all the things he wanted to accomplish and still have time for a social life. In fact, he even passed his schedule around to some of the other teammates and friends in order to help them get on track with their responsibilities. This method worked for Danny and his friends, who learned how important it is to separate friends from responsibilities.

Like Danny, when you go to college you are going to have to figure out how to strike a balance between having fun and having an appropriate amount of time and energy to read, study, and do other academic activities. Also like Danny, this may take a little bit of time to get right. Many students experience a dip in their grades their first semester of college. This drop in academic performance is due to many factors, such as the increased rigor of coursework, higher demands on your time for studying, being away from home, and all the social distractions of college life. However, the students that are able to figure out how to have some fun and also get their work done are the ones whose grades bounce back sooner rather than later.

Separating your friends from your responsibilities can be done in a number of ways. As Danny's story shows, creating a daily schedule can be extremely helpful. When creating your schedule, keep these tips in mind:[34]

1. Get into the habit of looking at your course schedules to identify what assignment due dates or exams are coming up. Course schedules will give you the approximate dates of all major assignments for the entire semester, so you can easily set up time in the weeks before due dates or exams to read, study, and do other work. Doing so will give you plenty of time to prepare yourself so you won't have to cram the night before something is due. It will also help you determine the periods during the semester when you will need to be diligent in separating your school responsibilities from your social life. Midterms and finals week are the two weeks of the semester when your schedule will likely be the most hectic when it comes to studying.

2. Plan ahead! Spreading out your workload is a much better approach than doing everything last minute. You'll produce better work, and you won't always be stressed out about how much work you have to do. If you have a paper due in two weeks, work on it a little bit each day for two weeks instead of having to spend all day and all night the day before it's due trying to get it done at the last minute. Spreading out your work time on assignments also prevents any unforeseen events from impacting your ability to finish your work. For example, if you wait until the night before an assignment is due to work on it and you get extremely sick, the likelihood of you finishing your assignment on time is greatly reduced. However, if you plan ahead, you can more easily work around things like that.

3. Make a checklist of everything you need to do each week. As you complete each task, mark it off your list. Having a checklist will keep you from forgetting to do an assignment, and the act of marking off each item will give you a sense of accomplishment and encourage you to keep going until all tasks are complete. It also serves as a quick

---

[34] "6 Time Management Tips for College Students," Rasmussen College, 18 June 2014, accessed 27 Jan 2015, http://www.rasmussen.edu/student-life/ blogs/college-life/time-management-tips-college/.

visual reminder of all the school work you have to do when your friends come calling to go out to dinner, a movie, or a party across campus. Being able to see what you need to accomplish in plain black and white can often help you make decisions that lead to better grades.

4. Build a schedule that is as consistent as possible. As Danny did, try breaking your day outside of class into one-hour blocks. Perhaps you study for three hours after your final class of the day, and then take an hour to have dinner with friends. Maybe then you study for two more hours, then take another hour off to socialize with other kids in your dorm. If your schedule is consistent, your body and mind will be able to understand better when it's time for work and when it's time for play. Your friends will also know when you're available to hang out or when you're studying if you keep a consistent schedule from day to day and week to week.

A key element of carving out an appropriate amount of time to study is to simply be honest with your friends. Saying no to a night out with your friends may lead you to feel guilty or feel as though you are ditching them or letting them down. But you need to let them know that you have to have certain times of the day to devote to your studies. Tell them your weekly schedule, and outline the times of the day that you will be unavailable. Again, having a schedule that is as consistent as possible will make this step much easier.

If you have a very busy academic week, tell your friends that they may not see you as much for a few days. If they are true friends, and if they are also devoted to their studies, they will completely understand. Being open and honest about your dedication to your studies is the best way to avoid situations in which you feel bad for ditching your friends. It also helps your friends better understand if they are being too demanding of your time.

Another good idea is to turn off your phone during the times of the day you've set aside for reading, studying, or doing other academic work. Nothing is more distracting than getting calls, texts, and notifications that someone has sent you a tweet or a message on Facebook. Although it may seem like you're only taking a second here and a second there

> *"Wherever there is a human being, I see God-given rights inherent in that being, whatever may be the sex or complexion."*
> –William Lloyd Garrison

to check your messages and notifications, over the course of an hour or two of studying, you can actually end up wasting a huge amount of time checking your phone. Turning it off eliminates that problem and helps you concentrate on your work.

Also, be wary of having Facebook and other social media sites open on your computer while you're doing research or writing a paper. The temptation is just too great to return that one email or check that one Facebook message. Just like with messages on your phone, these little distractions can add up and eat away at the time you've set aside to get your schoolwork done.

Your time to study needs to be free from these and other distractions so you can get your work done in a timely fashion. Remember, the faster you complete your homework, the more time you will have to spend with your friends! This doesn't mean that you should rush through your work, however. Keeping your head in the academic game with help you focus on your work, do a good job on it, and get the good grades you want and need.

There's no reason why you can't study with your friends either. If you and your roommate have the same math class, work together to get your work done. If you and your girlfriend have the same English professor, read the assigned texts together. You can make fun games to study for exams with your friends, quiz one another on important terms or topics, and critique one another's research papers. Studying with friends can be a big help because it makes the task of studying seem more fun and go by faster. Just be sure the focus is on the studying part!

Part of balancing your academic and social lives is to utilize fun with your friends as an incentive to get your studying done. For example, if you set aside 10 hours one week to work on a paper, reward yourself when the paper is done by spending time with your friends. If you're having an especially difficult time concentrating one day, bargain with yourself to get half of your reading done or three-quarters of your math assignment done, and then reward yourself by taking a break and talking with your roommate or spending time with your girlfriend. But just like studying should be time to study, time with friends shouldn't be interrupted by

> *"Black people cannot and will not become integrated into American society on any terms but those of self-determination and autonomy."*
>
> – Gerda Lerner

other tasks. Some people have trouble taking breaks from studying, so setting definite boundaries and giving your undivided attention to your friends during your time to be with them will keep your relationships in good standing and will also allow your body and mind to recharge from the drain of schoolwork.

You will likely find when you get to college that some of your friends just aren't the kind of people that will be good for you to be around. Maybe they get into the party scene, or maybe they simply don't do their work. You might have friends that spend all day and all night chasing girls, or you might have friends that get into the wrong crowd and start participating in illegal activities. Whatever the case, having friends in your life that take part in negative activities can still bring you and your grades down, even if you don't take part in their negative activities. Part of being an adult is making hard decisions. If your success in school is dependent upon making the decision to part ways with an out-of-control friend, that's something you must do! Doing so is one of the most difficult aspects of separating your friends from your responsibilities, but in the long run both you and your grades will be better off.

Having said that, you don't have to spend your entire college career with your face in a book in the library. Quite the contrary, college is about meeting new people, learning new things, and having fun experiences. The trick is to figure out how to balance all the demands on your time such that you get good grades and make good academic progress, while also forming and maintaining friendships and having some fun along the way too. You can't study 24-hours a day – nor should you. Part of keeping yourself motivated to learn is taking time away from learning to cut loose and have some fun.

If you find that you're having difficulties balancing your social life and your academic life, go back to Chapter 5 and re-read the section on time management. Review the tips for squeezing the most efficiency out of your time each day so you can accomplish as much as possible with the time you have. Also utilize the daily activity log at the end of Chapter 5 to help you identify how you're using your time and how you can make improvements on your time management.

CHAPTER 7

Making Your Dreams a Reality

Sometimes it's hard to visualize our dreams coming true. Sometimes this is because our dreams are too lofty – like being a billionaire or the best pro football player in history. Or maybe you have a difficult time imagining your dreams coming true because you have so many responsibilities to take care of, like paying the bills, providing for your family, or getting an education. Wherever you fall on that spectrum of thinking dreams don't come true, it's important to know that with hard work and dedication, your dreams (or a version of them) can become a reality.

Let's say that you love basketball and want to be a professional player in the NBA. Achieving that goal is not as easy as just being a gifted athlete. You have to put in the time and effort to get better, faster, and stronger. You have to get good grades in school so you can be eligible to play. You have to go to college and continue to learn and grow as a student and as an athlete in order to increase your chances of getting drafted into the NBA.

> *"The key is to keep company only with people who uplift you, whose presence calls forth your best."*
>
> – Epictetus

But as we discussed in Chapter 5, professional athletics is not your ticket to a better life. However, that doesn't mean that you can't still dream of a life that involves basketball. All it takes is an examination of your skills and abilities, and what you can do with them in order to build a career. If becoming an NBA player isn't in the cards, think about all the other jobs related to the NBA that you could potentially have. If you're interested in marketing or business, perhaps your dream changes to be involved in the business dealing of an NBA franchise. If you like science, maybe your dream changes to become a physical therapist so you can work with professional athletes on rehabilitating their bodies. Maybe you're drawn to studying human behavior, and you can become a sports psychologist to help athletes improve their performance. Or perhaps you get involved in scouting, coaching, or player development if you enjoy observing athletes and working directly with them.

So while you may have dreams that seem far too lofty, by changing your perspective and your expectations a little bit, you can still achieve a version of your ultimate dream that will bring you satisfaction and happiness in life. Making those adjustments also allows you to focus on a goal that is much more likely to be attained.

The same principle applies if you feel like there just isn't enough time in the day to work towards your dreams. This situation is best explained by the experience of Brian. Brian was always interested in becoming a teacher. He loved school and loved learning, and wanted more than anything to go to college and get his degree so he could teach elementary school. However, Brian had to work a part-time job after school and on the weekends in order to help support his family. Oftentimes Brian worked late into the night and didn't get enough sleep. From time to time he had trouble getting all his homework done because of all the time he spent at work.

> "If you don't like something, change it. If you can't change it, change your attitude. Don't complain."
> – Maya Angelou

However, Brian persevered and graduated high school with grades that were good enough to get him accepted to a local community college. But because of his responsibilities to help support his family, which included three younger siblings, Brian couldn't afford to go to college right away. Instead, he started working full-time at his job so he could make enough money to put some aside for his education.

Brian then started planning out how he could achieve his goal of being a teacher. He knew he needed experience working with kids, so on his off days from work he volunteered at a local kids club where he tutored elementary school kids in math and science. This allowed Brian to get some valuable experience working with children, and also allowed him to learn from a teacher that worked at the center. That teacher, Mrs. Robbins, was eager to answer Brian's questions about teaching and education. Seeing a spark in his eye that reminded her of her desire to become a teacher, she took Brian under her wing and worked with him on developing the skills he needed to be an effective teacher.

Brian also knew that he would need some financial assistance in order to afford college. He visited the campus of the local college that had accepted him for study and met with a financial aid advisor to go over the types of scholarships, grants, and loans for which he was qualified. He filled out all the applicable paperwork and filed it before the deadline to give himself the best chance of getting some money. Impressed by his dedication to volunteering at the kids club, a local organization selected Brian to receive a scholarship in the amount of $1,000 per semester. He also received a federal grant. Between the two, his tuition and fees for college would be covered, and he could use his own money to pay for books and supplies.

Once Brian was in college, the next step to achieving his goal was to focus on his studies and get good grades so he could transfer to a university and get his bachelor's degree. Brian reduced his hours at his job back to part-time so he could have more time to devote to his studies. Because he had learned to balance school, work, and family obligations, he was able to excel in his courses and graduated with his associate's degree with a 3.5 GPA.

From there, Brian went to a four-year college across town to finish his undergraduate degree. Eventually, Brian quit his job in favor of working part time as a paid tutor at the kids club, where his volunteer experience and his positive relationship with Mrs. Robbins got him the job. After two years of studying at his new college, Brian graduated with his de-gree in education and was hired to teach at the same school where he went as a boy. Finally, Brian had achieved his dream.

What Brian's story demonstrates is that dreams are not something you just think about. It takes a lot of hard work and effort in order to make them come true! In this chapter, you will explore what your dreams and goals are, and identify the steps you need to take in order to achieve your dreams. You will also explore the assets you have in your life – your interests, personal qualities, and people – that can help you reach your goals.

Step 1: Think about your dreams and your goals.

List five of your dreams. Dream the impossible dream and go for it!

_____

_____

_____

_____

_____

List five things that you struggle with, such as a school subject like math or a life skill like punctuality

_____

_____

_____

_____

_____

What is the common denominator between your short-comings?

_____
_____
_____
_____
_____

What have you learned from failure?

_____
_____
_____
_____
_____

Step 2: Write Down Your Goals

Identify five major goals you have for your life. These can relate to any area of life you want and can be as big or as small as you want.

_____
_____
_____

Your goals should prepare you to take MASSIVE ACTION to reach your dreams! List three goals you WILL accomplish within each time period below.

Within One Year
1.-

2.

3.

Within Three Years
1.

2.

3.

Within Five Years
1.

2.

3.

By setting attainable goals for yourself, you can more easily envision where you are and where you want to be. Sign and date below as a symbolic representation that this you will uphold this contract with yourself and work hard toward the goals you've outlined above.

(Your Signature) (Date)

Step 3: Your action plan to get where you want to go. Identify what it is you want in life, how you can get it, when you can get it, and who can help you along the way.

Who:

What:

How:

When:

Where:

Remember—Failing to plan is PLANNING to FAIL! You will never reach your goals and get where you want to be without first setting shortterm and long-term goals and identifying how you will achieve those goals!

Step 4: Research Careers—NOW!

List five things that you love to do.

1.
2.
3.
4.
5.

Now identify and list ten careers that are related to the five things you love to do.

1.
2.
3.
4.
5.
6.
7.
8.
9.
10.

Now make a list of all the people you know who work in these disciplines or career areas.

1.
2.
3.
4.
5.
6.
7.
8.
9.
10.

Call, email, and or write these people as soon as possible. Set up a time to meet with them so that you can ask questions and find out what they actually do on a daily basis. Ask lots of questions! What kind of hours do they work? Do they have health and medical insurance? What do they like most and least about their job? What training do they suggest that you seek to attain the highest level of certification? Don't be afraid to ask if you can be an intern for them and or shadow them. Getting some real life experience in each potential job area can help you clarify what it is you want to do with your life.

Step 5: The truth about achieving success and financial stability.

Success is all about what makes you happy. List five things that make you happy.

1.
2.
3.
4.
5.

List five reasons why the things listed above bring you happiness.

1.
2.
3.
4.
5.

List five people who have the success you desire.

1.
2.
3.
4.
5.

List five people who you admire and respect.

1.

2.

3.

4.

5.

Remember your income will be the average of your five closest friends or associates. SUCCESS leaves CLUES

Chapter 8

One Word: High School Graduation!

Are you thinking about going to college? Whether the decision has already been made or is still years away, please browse through my planner timeline, which we have designed to help you prepare for college. Please note that although you can complete most of the necessary tasks in your junior or senior years of high school, you should start planning as early as the eighth grade. Not only will this improve your chances of getting into the college of your choice, but it will also make applying much easier.

Below is a general guideline of steps you should follow while preparing for college.

Prepare for college early.

Preparing for college early may be vague advice, but is invaluable. Preparing early for your college education will help you position yourself to get into the college you want. I recommend that you start as early as the eighth grade, and start using the Student Planner in your freshman year of high school. Even if you are in your junior or senior year, you can still choose, apply, and get accepted to the college that is best for you if you plan carefully.

Regardless of the grade you are in now, there are some general notes to remember and rules to follow:

- Pay attention to deadlines and dates.
- Keep in mind that even though they may not be required for high school graduation, most colleges require at least three, and

often prefer four, years of studies in math, English, science, and social studies.

> *"Setting goals is the first step in turning the invisible into the visible."*
> – Tony Robbin

- In addition to this, most colleges require at least two years of the same foreign language.
- Your grades are important but the difficulty of your coursework can also be a significant factor in a college's decision to admit you. In general, most colleges prefer students with average grades in tougher courses than students who opt for an easy.
- You should also note that most high schools grade AP courses on a 5 point scale rather than the 4 point scale used for other classes, essentially giving students a bonus point for tackling the extra difficulty (e.g., a B in an AP course is worth as much as an A in a non-AP course).
- College admission officers will pay the closest attention to your GPA, class rank, college credit, AP courses, and scores on standardized tests.
- Participation in extracurricular activities is also a good idea in high school. Activities that require time and effort outside the classroom (such as speech and debate, band, communications, and drama) indicate a willingness to cooperate with others and put forth the effort needed to succeed.
- Computer science courses or courses that require students to use computers in research and project preparation can also help aid your future college performance.

Choosing a career and a corresponding major will help you decide which colleges are right for you.

1. Find the college that's right for you.

There are multiple ways you can select a college.

- By name
- Preference of study (discipline)
- Geography

2. Visit the college(s) of your choice.

Once you have narrowed your selection, arrange to visit the campuses in person.

3. Discover your payment options.

You should look into scholarships, student loans, and other financial aid options before you apply to a particular college or university. Since there is so much financial aid available, however, and since colleges are generally willing to work with you to put together a favorable financial aid package, money shouldn't be a primary concern when considering a college.

4. Apply online.

5. Come back in January for financial aid assistance.

In January, is a good time to start completing the financial aid assistance applications for most post secondary insti-tutions. Your high school counselor will help you complete your FAFSA and teach you other ways to for college.

Grade 8

Following are the steps you should take at each grade level starting with 8th grade to prepare yourself for the college experience.

- Talk to your guidance counselor (or teachers, if you don't have access to a guidance counselor) about the following:
- Going to a four-year college or university
- Courses to start taking in the 9th grade
- The importance colleges and universities place on grades, and what year in school grades will start to be considered in the admissions process
- College preparatory classes you should be taking in high school (9th through 12th grade)

- Academic enrichment programs (including summer and weekend programs) available through your school or local colleges

Remember, you will have more options if you start planning now and keep your grades up.

- Think about pursuing extracurricular activities (such as sports, performing arts, volunteer work, or other activities that interest you).

Grade 9/Freshman Year

- Talk to your guidance counselor (or teachers, if you don't have access to a guidance counselor) about the following:
  - Attending a four-year college or university
  - Establishing your college preparatory classes; your schedule should consist of at least 4 college preparatory classes per year, including:
    - 4 years of English
    - 3 years of math (through Algebra II or trigonometry)
    - 2 years of foreign language
    - 2 years of natural science
    - 2 years of history/social studies
    - 1 year of art
    - 1 year of electives from the above list
  - Using the Student Planner to keep track of your courses and grades.
  - Enrolling in algebra or geometry classes and a foreign language for both semesters (most colleges have math and foreign language requirements)

Remember, you will have more options if you start planning now for college and keep your grades up.

- Create a file of the following documents and notes:
  - Copies of report cards
  - List of awards and honors

- List of school and community activities in which you are involved, including both paid and volunteer work, and descriptions of what you do.

- Start thinking about the colleges you want to attend. Once you have narrowed down the list of colleges and universities in which you are interested, start touring the campuses.

Grade 10/Sophomore Year

- Talk to your guidance counselor (or teachers, if you don't have access to a guidance counselor) about the following:

> *"Knowing is not enough; we must apply. Willing is not enough; we must do."*
> – Johann Wolfgang von Goethe

- Reviewing the high school curriculum needed to satisfy the requirements of the colleges you are interested in attending
- Finding out about AP (Advanced Placement) courses:
  - What courses are available
  - Whether or not you are eligible for the classes that you want to take
  - How to enroll in them for your junior year
- Update your file, or start one if you haven't already. (See Grade 9 for a list of what it should contain.)
- Continue extracurricular activities, as admissions officers look at students' extracurricular activities when considering them for admission.
- Continue participation in academic enrichment programs, summer workshops, and camps with specialty focuses such as music, arts, science, etc.
- Take the PSAT in October. The scores will not count for National Merit Scholar consideration in your sophomore year, but it is valuable practice for when you take the PSAT again in your junior year (when the scores will count), as well as for the SAT I exam which you should also be taking in your junior

year. You will receive your PSAT results in December. Don't forget to start preparing for the SAT.
- Register, in April, for the SAT II for any subjects you will be completing before June.
- Take the SAT II in June.

Grade 11/Junior Year Fall Semester

- Maintaining your grades during your junior year is especially important. You should be doing at least 2 hours of homework each night and participating in study groups.
- Talk to your guidance counselor (or teachers, if you don't have access to a guidance counselor) about the following:
  - Availability of and enrollment in AP classes
  - Schedules for the PSAT, SAT I and II, ACT, and AP exams
  - Discuss why you should take these exams and how they could benefit you.
  - Determine which exams you will take. (You can always change your mind.)
  - Sign up and prepare for the exams you've decided to take.
  - Ask for a preview of your academic record and profile, determine what gaps or weaknesses there are, and get suggestions on how to strengthen your candidacy for the schools in which you are interested.
  - Determine what it takes to gain admission to the college(s) of your choice, in addition to GPA and test score requirements.
- **August:**
  - Obtain schedules and forms for the SAT I, SAT II, ACT, and AP exams.
- **September:**
  - Register for the PSAT exam offered in October. Remember that when you take the PSAT in your junior year, the scores will count towards the National Achievement Program (and it is good practice for the SAT I).

- **October**:
  - Take the PSAT. Narrow your list of colleges to include a few colleges with requirements at your current GPA, a few with requirements above your current GPA, and at least one with requirements below your GPA. Your list should contain approximately 8-12 schools you are seriously considering. Start researching your financial aid options as well.
  - Begin scheduling interviews with admissions counselors. If possible, schedule tours of the school grounds on the same days. You and your parent(s) may want to visit the colleges and universities during spring break and summer vacation, so that you do not have to miss school. Some high schools consider a campus visit an excused absence; however, you may be able to schedule interviews and visits during the school year, without incurring any penalties.
- **November:**
  - Review your PSAT results with your counselor, in order to identify your strengths and to determine the areas that you may need to improve upon.
- **December:**
  - You will receive your scores from the October PSAT. Depending on the results, you may want to consider signing up for free online SAT prep. Many high schools offer short-term preparatory classes or seminars on the various exams, which tell the students what to expect and can actually help to boost their scores.

Spring Semester

- **January:**
  - Take Campus Tours online or in person to further narrow your list of colleges to match your personality, GPA, and test scores.
- **February:**
  - Register for the March SAT and/or the April ACT tests. Find out from each college the deadlines for applying for admission and which tests to take. Make sure your test dates give college's ample time to receive test scores. It is a good idea to take the SAT and/or ACT in the spring to allow you time to review your results and retake the exams in the fall of your senior year, if necessary.

- **March:**
  - Take the March SAT I exam.
  - If you are interested in taking any AP exam(s), you should sign up for the exam(s) at this time. If your school does not offer the AP exams, check with your guidance counselor to determine schools in the area that do administer the exam(s), as well as the dates and times that the exam(s) you are taking will be offered. Scoring well on the AP exam can sometimes earn you college credit.
- **April:**
  - Take the April ACT test.
- **May:**
  - Take AP, SAT I, and SAT II exams.
  - Talk to teachers about writing letters of recommendation for you. Think about what you would like included in these letters (how you would like to be presented) and politely ask your teachers if they can accommodate you.
- **June:**
  - Add any new report cards, test scores, honors, or awards to your file. Visit colleges. Call ahead for appointments with financial aid, admissions, and academic advisors at the college(s) in which you are most interested. During your visits, talk to professors, sit in on classes, spend a night in the dorms, and speak to students about the college(s). Doing these things will allow you to gather the most information about the college and the atmosphere in which you would be living, should you choose to attend. Some colleges have preview programs that allow you to do all of these. Find out which of the schools that you will be visiting offer these programs and take advantage of them.
  - Take the SAT I, SAT II, and the ACT tests.
  - If you go on interviews or visits, don't forget to send thank you notes.

> *"Determine never to be idle. No person will have occasion to complain of the want of time who never loses any. It is wonderful how much may be done if we are always doing."*
>
> – Thomas Jefferson

Summer Between Junior and Senior Years

- Practice writing online applications and filling out rough drafts of each application, without submitting them. Focus on the essay portions of these applications, deciding how you would like to present yourself. Don't forget to mention your activities outside of school.
- Review your applications, especially the essays. Ask family, friends, and teachers to review your essays for grammar, punctuation, readability, and content.

Decide if you are going to apply under a particular college's early decision or early action programs. This requires you to submit your applications early, typically between October and December of your senior year, but offers the benefit of receiving the college's decision concerning your admission early, usually before January 1. If you choose to apply early, you should do so for the college/university that is your first choice in schools to attend. Many early decision programs are legally binding, requiring you to attend the college you are applying to, should they accept you.

Read your college mail and send reply cards to your schools of interest.

Grade 12/Senior Year Fall Semester

- **September:**

  - Check your transcripts to make sure you have all the credits you need to get into your college(s) of choice. Find out from the colleges to which you are applying whether or not they need official copies of your transcripts (transcripts sent directly from your high school) sent at the time of application.

  - Register for October/November SAT I, SAT II, and ACT tests. If you haven't already done it, sign up for the free online test prep.

  - Take another look at your list of colleges, and make sure that they still satisfy your requirements. Add and/or remove colleges as necessary.

- Make sure you meet the requirements (including any transcript requirements) for all the colleges to which you want to apply. Double-check the deadlines, and take massive action and apply.

- Give any recommendation forms to the appropriate teachers or counselors with stamped, college-addressed, envelopes making certain that your portion of the forms are filled out completely and accurately.

- Most early decision and early action applications are due between October 1 and November 1. Keep this in mind if you intend to take advantage of these options and remember to request that your high school send your official transcripts to the college to which you are applying.

- **October:**

- Make a final list of schools that interest you and keep a file of deadlines and required admission items for each school.

- Take SAT and/or ACT tests. Have the official scores sent by the testing agency to the colleges/ universities that have made your final list of schools. Register for December or January SAT I and/or SAT II tests, if necessary.

> "Well done is better than well said."
> – Benjamin Franklin

- Continue thinking about and beginning writing (if you have not already started) any essays to be included with your applications.

- **November:**

- Submit your college admission applications on time.

- **December:**

- Early decision replies usually arrive between December 1st and December 31st.

- If you haven't already done so, make sure your official test scores are being sent to the colleges to which you are applying.

- Schedule any remaining required interviews.

Spring Semester

- **January:**

- Complete and submit your college financial aid application and the Free Application for Student Financial Aid (FAFSA) between January 1 and February 15, and check for other financial aid options. (In other words, Get Money.) In order to be considered for financial aid, you will need to submit these forms even if you have not yet been notified of your acceptance to the college(s) to which you applied.

- Go to the FAFSA on the Web. If you do not have internet go to your public library.

- Request that your high school send your official transcripts to the colleges to which you are applying.

- Make sure your parents have completed their income tax forms in anticipation of the financial aid applications.

- Contact the admissions office of the college(s) to which you have applied to make sure that your information has been received, and that they have everything they need from you.

- **February:**

- If you completed the FAFSA, you should receive your Student Aid Report (SAR) within four weeks. Make the necessary corrections and return it to the FAFSA processor.

- Complete your scholarship applications.

- Contact the financial aid office of the college(s) to which you have applied to make sure that your information has been received, and that they have everything they need from you.

- **March/April:**

- You will probably hear from the colleges as to whether or not you are accepted by April 15.

- Compare your acceptance letters, financial aid and scholarship offers.

- When you choose a college that has accepted you, you will be required to pay a nonrefundable deposit for freshman tuition (this should ensure your place in the entering freshman class).

- Compare financial aid packages and options.

- **May:**

- Take AP exams for any AP subjects you studied in high school.

- You should make a decision by May 1st as to which college you will be attending and notify the school by mailing your commitment deposit check. Many schools require that your notification letter be postmarked by this date.
- If you were placed on a waiting list for a particular college, and have decided to wait for an opening, contact that college and let them know you are still very interested.

- **June:**

- Have your school send your final transcripts to the college which you will be attending.
- Contact your college to determine when fees for tuition, room and board are due and how much they will be.

- **Summer After Senior Year**

- Participate in any summer orientation programs for incoming freshmen

CHAPTER 8

Make your college acceptance a reality

Steps to Financial Aid

By the fall of your senior year in high school, you should have chosen the colleges, to which you'll apply, and:

- Determined their costs of attendance.
- Now you are ready to take the next steps.

For some students, having made their college choices and having determined based on the total cost of attendance that their families will not be eligible for financial aid based on demonstrated financial need, the next step is either to check out payment plans and/or non-need-based merit scholarships offered by colleges, to look into non-need-based loans, or consult the free scholarship search.

> "If you start by promising what you don't even have yet, you'll lose your desire to work towards getting it."
> – Paulo Coelho

For the vast majority of you who are eligible for needbased financial aid, the steps below will help you apply for financial aid.

1. **Find out and comply with each college's admission and financial aid application deadlines.** Don't jeopardize your chances for receiving aid by not filing applications on time. Use your personal calendar to keep track of the many deadlines.

2. **Review your scholarship checklist and gather and complete the necessary forms; meet the deadlines.**

3. **Complete the Free Application for Federal Student Aid (FAFSA) in order to qualify for aid through the federal government.**

- This site gives you access to the FAFSA. You'll save time in getting the information to colleges and state scholarship programs.
- You can file the FAFSA any time after January 1 of the year you will enter college, but I recommend you file it no later than February 15 (remember, using estimated income figures is allowed).
- Be sure all the required signatures accompany the application.

3. If your college choices require copies of parent income tax forms, be sure to submit them as soon after January 1 as they are completed.
4. The federal government has two programs to reduce the amount of income tax owed by moderate-income families with students pursuing undergraduate study.

> *"If you want to conquer fear, don't sit home and think about it. Go out and get busy."*
> – Dale Carnegie

- **Hope Tax Credit:** This plan is for families with students in the first two years of an undergraduate study program. A tax credit of up to $1500 per year can be claimed for each family member enrolled at least half time during those years. The amount of the credit is based on the family's income and is phased out at higher incomes.

- **Lifetime Learning Tax Credit:** This credit applies to all eligible family members being claimed by the taxpayer and taking courses at an eligible school. Families can claim up to 20% of tuition and fees—up to a maximum of $1000 per entire family per year. This tax credit is phased out at higher income levels.

5. **If required by your college choices, complete the College Board PROFILE application for financial aid.**

- Contact your colleges to find out if they are among those requiring the PROFILE application for financial aid (approximately 350 colleges nationwide).

- PROFILE forms are available in your guidance office or from the colleges which require it.
- Be sure all the required signatures accompany the application.

6. **Complete any additional college-specific financial aid forms that may be required.**

- Contact your college for the college-specific financial aid forms.

7. **Review the Student Aid Report (SAR) you'll receive on the basis of your completed FAFSA.**

- You should receive your SAR within four weeks of submitting the FAFSA. Look for the government's figure for expected family contribution and the listing of the data you supplied.
- If you find any errors in your data, make the corrections and return the form as soon as possible so that your college choices receive the correct information.

8. **Review the CSS Acknowledgment you'll receive once your PROFILE application has been processed.**

- Compare the acknowledgment's data confirmation section with the data you provided.
- If you need to make changes or corrections to the PROFILE data, submit the changes directly to the appropriate college financial aid offices.
- Review the list of colleges and programs that will be receiving the PROFILE data, and add additional colleges if you wish.

9. **Review financial aid award packages**

- Be sure you know the deadlines for accepting your aid offers: you don't want to procrastinate the review past the deadline for getting any aid at all!
- Review each award carefully.
- If you receive more than one financial aid award, be sure to compare them.

10. **Remember it's not just about the sticker price, the bottom line, and the grant/loan ratio.**

- Your college choice will have a tremendous impact on your future. You are beginning a lifelong intellectual, cultural, and social adventure. Choose wisely.

Do You Need A Typical Award Package?

If your application for admission has been accepted, and you have taken all the steps to apply for financial aid, and your family demonstrates financial need, you are likely to receive a financial aid award.

Now what?

Interpreting a financial aid award letter fully takes some time. While most colleges try to make their awards as clear as possible, you may still have questions. You will want to get them answered before the deadline to accept the financial aid award

The following sample award may help you interpret you own aid awards.

Total Cost of Attendance	$20,000
Expected Family Contribution	$5,000
Outside Scholarship	$1,000
Financial Need	$14,000
Federal Pell Grant	$0
State Scholarship Grant	$1,500
Institutional Grant	$7,500
Federal Perkins Loan	$1,500
Federal Direct Loan	$1,500
Federal Work Study	$2,000
Total Award	$14,000

In this award, the college is covering more than half of the demonstrated financial need with a grant. That certainly helps! But it would be important to ask the financial aid staff whether this level of grant can be expected in future years. (Unfortunately, some colleges do make large initial grants to encourage students to enroll, and may reduce or remove grants after the first year.) You'll also want to ask about the continued availability of the state grant.

If the grants look to be stable over the time you'd be enrolled, you can estimate the total student loan indebtedness you would have after four years—in this case, around

$12,000 if college costs remain the same. That's about the average level of indebtedness for students graduating nationwide. Research or call the school financial aid office to see what the average monthly payments on these loans would be, depending on the interest rate.

You'll also want to look at the work-study figure. Are you willing to work on campus to earn these funds? If not, you will be expected to come up with the $2,000 in some other way (either extra work beyond the summer earnings expectation, a gift from a relative, a loan, etc.).

Of course, if you have received more than one financial aid award, you will want to compare them.

How do I compare award packages?

If you've received more than one financial aid award package, this module will help you compare them. Here are some points you'll want to consider:

- **Ratio of grant to loan**

In general, packages with higher percentages of grant aid than loan aid will be more appealing. You'll have less to pay while in college and fewer debts to repay when you graduate. This ratio may also give you a clue as to how much the college wants you, since colleges tend to award higher proportions of grant aid to the most desirable students in the accepted group.

- **Ratio of self help to grant**

This looks at the big picture beyond just grant vs. loan. How much of the total cost of attendance are you expected to cover through loans, the expected family contribution, and student employment on campus? You'll need to be realistic about whether you can meet the earnings expectations.

- **Loan terms**

Compare the types of loans you are expected to take on. Are the terms favorable in terms of interest and repayment? Student loans with low interest rates and no repayment until after college are preferable to private or unsubsidized loans with less attractive terms.

- **Gapping**

Some colleges award aid that amounts to less than the difference between the Expected Family Contribution and the total cost of attendance. If you find you have been gapped in an award, only you can determine if you will be able to, and want to, come up with the additional money in order to attend.

Future Packages

You'll want to find out if all or part of your financial aid award is renewable if family circumstances stay the same (or worsen!). Beware of packages that seem too good to be true: often the terms will not be as favorable for subsequent years of enrollment.

- **Outside Scholarships**

If you are applying for or will otherwise qualify for outside scholarships, be sure to find out how this money will be treated in each college's financial aid award package. At some colleges, an outside scholarship directly reduces the institutional grant by the same amount. Other colleges allow a certain amount to go first against any suggested loan, then, if the outside scholarship is greater than that amount, it will reduce equally institutional grant and loan.

> *"Go for it now. The future is promised to no one."*
> – Wayne Dyer

EPILOGUE

I should not be here right now, I should be dead. 12 years ago thanksgiving in 2006 I received the scare of my life. I almost died because of a 9 pound tumor on my intestines. The issue I have is if I would have died, I would not be here on this earth to share my thoughts with you.

I want you to know that I am writing this book for you. I want you to defy the odds and reach for the stars and be all that you can be. Never let anyone or a statistical program put any limits on you and determine what your destination in life should be. I urge you to be all that you can be and take your passion and energy and TAKE MASSIVE ACTION towards the Goals, DREAMS and DESIRES that are within you.

Make no bones about it the road will be hard and sometimes lonely, but YOU who preservers with tenacity and grit will have all your heart desires. But the key to your success lies in the words below. "Do today what others won't so you can have tomorrow what others don't"
–Pat Dunne

Why, because **I was just like YOU!** Young, poor single-parent home, labeled ADHD from the hood... But I MADE IT! And so can **YOU!**

ABOUT ME

MDonnell Tenner M.ED, was born in Chicago, and raised via Lambert, Mississippi and East Saint Paul, Minnesota. The only boy in a family with three sisters, he learned early on in life about having a strong work ethic and how education is the key foundation to success. His strong faith in God and a willingness to understand from whence he came, kept him grounded and determined to never stop uplifting the urban communities. He also is a descendant of the Cherokee Indian nation.

His strength comes from his mother and father who enlisted in the army to help provide for him and his siblings even though his divorced when he was only 5 years old. At fourteen years old, he forged his birth certificate and worked forty hours or more a week in the summers so his mother would not have to provide for his school clothes, athletic fees and equipment.

Upon graduating from high school, Tenner was able to keep his focus on education while playing collegiate football. He received a degree in sports management with a minor in business administration. He went on to earn his Master's degree in educational administration from Saint Mary's University of Minnesota. Mr. Tenner also holds K-12 Principal certification and Superintendency certification. He currently is finishing his Doctoral studies a Nova South Eastern University in Florida. MDonnell Tenner motto is "Chances Make Champions." He will not rest until all children, whatever race, color and or creed, are getting equitable education experiences and the Achievement Gap is permanently significantly closed."

MDonnell Tenner is a proud member of Omega Psi Phi Fraternity Inc. He is a gifted motivational speaker, mentor, educational leader, and author, as well as a proven creative "out-of-the–box" educator who gets results. His future goal is to make official visits to all at-risk school districts throughout the nation, empowering them through motivational talks and workshops.

MDONNELL TENNER, M.ED
240 Ways Series Presents

240 Ways
To Close
The
Achievement
Gap
$19.95
Qty:_____

240 Ways Presents

The Other Walking Dead: Plights & Strategies for the Urban K12 Male

$24.95
Qty:_____

240 Ways To Close The Achievement Gap

Teachers Only w/ Reflection Guide Manual

$39.95
Qty:_____

ORDER BY:
240 Ways Series LLC
Suite 111
Hollow Brook Dr. 63034
www.240waysseries.com

314.443.8776

Name _____
Company_____
Email _____
Tel# _____
Address_____
City_____State_____

Payment By:

☐ Check (Payable to M. Donnell Tenner)

☐ Mastercard ☐ Amex ☐ Visa

Credit Card#_____Exp. Date _____

Print Name as it appears on Card
_____

Signature:_____

Date_____

Subtotal_____

S&H_____

Total_____

Do you know of any K-12 Organizations that may be interested in having MDonnell Tenner, M.ED as a Guest Speaker? Presenting 1/2 Day Workshops on building meaningful relationships with diverse students.

Name _____

Organization _____

Email _____

Tel _____

Available October 1st, 2018

24 Laws of Power

Success For Urban Educators

WWW.240WaysSeries.com

Made in the USA
Monee, IL
26 August 2020